SpringerBriefs in Information Systems

Series editor

Jörg Becker

More information about this series at http://www.springer.com/series/10189

Rocco Agrifoglio

Knowledge Preservation Through Community of Practice

Theoretical Issues and Empirical Evidence

 Springer

Rocco Agrifoglio
Department of Management, Accounting
    and Economics
University of Naples "Parthenope"
Naples
Italy

ISSN 2192-4929   ISSN 2192-4937   (electronic)
SpringerBriefs in Information Systems
ISBN 978-3-319-22233-2   ISBN 978-3-319-22234-9   (eBook)
DOI 10.1007/978-3-319-22234-9

Library of Congress Control Number: 2015945332

Springer Cham Heidelberg New York Dordrecht London

Springer International Publishing AG Switzerland is part of Springer Science+Business Media
(www.springer.com)

To Valeria, who inspires me every day
to live a life worth living, and to the little
boy who is coming to brighten our lives

Foreword

A community of practice is viewed as a group of people informally connected by shared expertise and a common interest in a particular domain or area. It is recognized as an effective organizational form because it enables members to share their experiences and knowledge in spontaneous, flowing, and creative ways. In comparison with existing organizational structures, such as teams, work groups, and business units, it provides an alternative and simpler approach to knowledge management. Communities of practice are self-organizing systems, whose methods of interaction, rules, and life span are determined by community members without constraints of time and space. Such communities are particularly suitable for exchanging and sharing knowledge among their members, because of their integral systems of social relationships and engagement in working activities.

The perspectives in more recent literature on situated learning and practice have superseded those of the pioneering contributions by moving the focus of research from the "geographies" of organization (co-location/distribution) to dimensions of social interaction and collaboration. In this respect, a community of practice can be viewed as a knowledge network in which location, proximity, and distance are determined by relationship rather than geography. Building upon the economic and organizational literature, such communities seem to be an "intermediate" or "hybrid" form in respect of "hierarchy" and "market." In particular, a community of practice may be interpreted as a particular form of social network, where social coordination and control mechanisms—in terms of social norms, reputation and peer control—are critical for the development, maintenance, and exploitation of knowledge.

In respect of previous research on knowledge management, and on issues of knowledge creation and sharing in particular, this book aims to explore the process of knowledge preservation in a community of practice. The topic is critical for information systems research and organizational literature, since knowledge preservation is not an obvious and predictable process in organizations, but needs to be carefully designed. Organizations are often busy acquiring and exploiting technological knowledge, but forget that such knowledge remains in the heads of the employees if it is not institutionalized in the structure of the organization.

Moreover, knowledge codification and articulation is not always feasible in organizations due to the variety in the forms of knowledge and in the established ways of managing it. Community of practice represents a natural setting enabling members to preserve the various forms of knowledge in organizations. In this regard, it can be viewed as one of the most suitable ways to avoid the loss of knowledge in an organization. However, although the literature recognizes community of practice as critical to knowledge preservation, the different ways in which a community preserves the various forms of knowledge merits deeper investigation.

Chapter 1 reviews the literature on organizational knowledge, highlighting its epistemological and ontological dimensions and the processes of knowledge management. It also explores the various mechanisms and tools that enable employers to create, share, and preserve knowledge in organizations.

Chapter 2 investigates the idea of community of practice by focusing particularly on the different types and main characteristics in terms of domain, community, and practice. It also introduces the topic of knowledge preservation, pointing out the processes of knowledge management, and of knowledge creation, sharing, and preservation in particular, in a community of practice.

Chapter 3 links the literature on knowledge management and research on community of practice in order to understand how a community preserves knowledge over time and space. Building upon practice-based literature, I propose a dynamic framework for analyzing the "community knowledge preservation" process, identifying the various mechanisms and tools that enable a community of practice to select, store, and actualize the explicit and tacit forms of collective knowledge.

Finally, Chap. 4 reports four case studies on communities of practice: the scientific community of the ItAIS, the religious communities of Guardia Sanframondi and Palermo, and the WoodenBoat community. These studies provide empirical evidence on various mechanisms and tools that allow members to preserve explicit and tacit forms of collective knowledge in a community of practice.

Understanding the working rules in communities of practice can be extremely useful in predicting future forms of work organization, including in the domains of entrepreneurship and management. Individual attitudes and habits with regard to collaborative work, even among people which are connected by weak ties, seem to be innate skills among "digital natives," who have always been able to use information technologies and systems, now all-pervasive, in design and decision making.

These assumptions lead us to believe that, before long, the community of practice could be recognized as an "ancestor" to which people will refer in explaining how new forms of business and work organization have evolved. Also from this point of view, the volume of Rocco Agrifoglio offers useful and original contributions to the debate on organizational theories.

Naples   Prof. Marcello Martinez
June 2015   Second University of Naples

Preface

Since time began, people have always wanted to expand the boundaries of their knowledge. The knowledge they possessed was exploited for scientific and technological advancement, because of the considerable effects of science and technology on the development of any society. The stone wheel, the law of universal gravitation, penicillin, the steam engine, etc., are just some of the greatest achievements of mankind. However, the knowledge that was developed was not always passed down to future generations. History is full of examples where people build artifacts that are useful to their work, but forget about those already built. As in the past, individuals, organizations, and communities are today very busy exploiting acquired knowledge to develop new knowledge, without considering that the latter is not risk free and they may lose track of it over time. Indeed, knowledge that remains in the heads of the employees, rather than being institutionalized within the organization, can represent a severe threat to a firm due to the failure to transfer such knowledge from individual to corporate memory. This problem is of growing concern in knowledge management research, which is striving to identify technologies and infrastructures able to avoid the loss of organizational knowledge. Among these, community of practice has been recognized as one of the most suitable ways to structure and process the various forms of knowledge in organizations.

Communities of practice have always and still do exist everywhere in every aspect of human life. We all belong to a number of them—at work, at school, at home, in our hobbies. They are a natural setting where cultivating practice enables members to develop and share knowledge while also, because it is socially constructed, institutionalizing it within the organizational structure. Practice in a social context, and in a community of practice in particular, comes from and contributes to knowledge, thanks to the interaction that community members have with the world. This assumption leads us to distinguish between "knowledge" (as possession) and "knowing" (as action), so opening an academic debate on the interplay between them and on the effects of this interplay on the preservation of knowledge.

This book links knowledge management literature and Information Systems (IS) research to explore the process of knowledge preservation within a community of practice. It contributes to existing literature in different ways. First, I conceptualize "community knowledge preservation," i.e., "the process of maintaining knowledge crucial to a community of practice by storing knowledge and activities over time and providing members with the possibility of recall for the future." In contrast to previous knowledge management research, knowledge preservation is thus viewed as a process in its own right rather than an integral part of knowledge creation and sharing. Furthermore, I also investigate how communities of practice preserve knowledge, by identifying the main mechanisms and tools enabling members to select, store, and actualize the explicit and tacit forms of collective knowledge.

The book is organized as follows. Chapter 1 explores issues of organizational knowledge by stressing its epistemological (explicit and tacit) and ontological (individual and collective) dimensions. It also explains the knowledge management processes by distinguishing between knowledge creation, sharing, and preservation. Chapter 2 reviews the literature on community of practice and addresses some of the challenges identified in studies on knowledge management. Chapter 3 highlights the process of knowledge preservation within a community of practice and identifies the mechanisms and tools that enable members to select, store, and actualize explicit and tacit forms of collective knowledge. Finally, Chap. 4 provides evidence drawn from four communities of practice, where different mechanisms and tools allow members to preserve explicit and tacit forms of collective knowledge.

This book, like all others, is not the product of one individual, but arises from a joint effort by many people. The ideas and concepts rooted in this book came from observation of, and discussion with, various colleagues and friends who shared my passion for this amazing topic. I have had the good fortune to interact with many academics and practitioners across the world who have influenced my thinking over the years. Among the most influential, I want to acknowledge Christian Rauscher (Senior Editor of Springer—Business/Economics), who has supported me through all phases of publication. I wish also to express my gratitude to Drs. Isidro Peña Garcia-Pardo and Mario Javier Donate Manzanares, who invited me to the UCLM in Ciudad Real, Spain, as visiting researcher, and to Professors Marco De Marco and Cecilia Rossignoli, Drs. Paolo Spagnoletti, Alessio Maria Braccini, and Stefano Za, and all the ItAIS community members. Each of them has provided indispensable suggestions and valuable advice, which has led me to develop and refine on the theoretical speculations and the empirical case studies in this book.

I would like to acknowledge my colleagues at the University of Naples "Parthenope": Professors Filomena Buonocore and Luisa Varriale and Drs. Mauro Romanelli, Domenico Salvatore, and Paola Briganti, who all helped to teach me and ultimately helped inspire this book. Moreover, special thanks go to Professor Concetta Metallo and Dr. Francesco Schiavone for their engagement and support in planning and developing the contents of this book over the years.

Last, but certainly not least, I would like to add a special mention of Professor Marcello Martinez, to whom I am very grateful for having written the book's Foreword, and Professor Maria Ferrara, who has been an important source of suggestions and guidance.

Naples   Rocco Agrifoglio
June 2015

Contents

Chapter 1
Preserving Knowledge in Organizations

Abstract This chapter aims to explore the issue of knowledge in organizations. After reviewing the literature on the meanings of knowledge, the study focuses on organizational knowledge and its taxonomy, distinguishing between epistemological (explicit and tacit) and ontological (individual and collective) dimensions. This chapter also highlights the knowledge management paradigm, identifying the various processes, mechanisms and tools that enable people to create, share and preserve knowledge in organizations.

Keywords Organizational knowledge · Explicit and tacit knowledge · Individual and collective knowledge · Knowledge management · Knowledge management processes

1.1 Defining Knowledge

What is knowledge? Defining knowledge is a matter of ongoing debate among academics from different disciplines and positions. According to Nonaka (1994, p. 15), "Knowledge is a multifaceted concept with multilayered meanings." Knowledge represents a complex topic which, being abstract, is difficult to define and quantify. In any organizational settings knowledge tends to be fuzzy in nature and is usually deeply and closely attached to the individuals who hold it (Davenport and Prusak 1998). It is therefore challenging to define, measure and manage (Ipe 2003). For this reason, scholars usually tend to focus on the more measurable components of knowledge, such as the attributes and variables of any knowledge development activity through which the same knowledge manifests itself.

Since the classical Greek era, knowledge, as a broad and abstract concept, has stimulated wide epistemological debates in western philosophy. Polanyi (1958, 1962) tries to trace the major milestones of the epistemological debate, identifying the main perspectives that focus on the conceptualization of knowledge, such as those of rationalism (advanced by philosophers such as Descartes in the 17th century), empiricism (advanced by Locke and others in the 18th century), and interactionism (advanced by Kant and others in the 19th century). Without going into too much detail, as this would not be relevant for our research purposes, it has been assumed that traditional epistemology mainly focuses on "truthfulness" as the essential attribute of knowledge, emphasizing the absolute, static and nonhuman nature of knowledge, which can typically be expressed in propositional structures in formal logic.

Unlike Greek philosophy, more recent literature views knowledge as "a dynamic human process of justifying personal beliefs as part of an aspiration for the truth" (Nonaka 1994, p. 15). Specifically, according to Nonaka (1994) and Huber (1991), knowledge is conceived as the specific and justified belief of an individual, which is able to increase his/her capacity to take effective action. In this context, taking action depends on several factors, such as physical skills and competencies (e.g., when playing football or doing handicraft), cognitive/intellectual activity (e.g., problem solving), or both (e.g., in surgery, which requires both manual skills and cognitive knowledge of human anatomy and medicine). Otherwise, in literature, knowledge is interpreted as core competencies (Hamel and Prahalad 1990), skills (Stewart 1997), values and norms (Leonard-Barton 1992), and information (Schwartz et al. 2000). Often these terms are used interchangeably (Bell 1979), which is an unpleasant complication for operational managers (Wijnhoven 2003). At the same time, a lot of what is popularly called knowledge refers to effective behavior or skills and not to explicit understanding or representation (Wijnhoven 2003).

As explained above, researchers from different fields have attempted to define and measure knowledge by using various theories, methods and tools. For instance, Information Systems (IS) researchers try to define knowledge mainly by making a distinction between knowledge, information and data. In particular, information is a flow of messages or meanings which might be able to enrich, restructure or change knowledge, while knowledge is the result of a process of creation and management by the flow of information, related to the commitment and beliefs of its holder (e.g., Dretske 1981; Machlup 1983; Vance 1997). In this regard, human agency is crucial in processing information into knowledge. Also, as suggested by Maglitta (1996), data are raw numbers and facts, while information is processed data, and knowledge is "information made actionable." In this perspective, the terms are conceptualized according to the differences among them, which are clarified when information becomes knowledge. Thus, the three terms are deeply linked and each one is the result of a significant change in the previous step in respect of the following structure: data, information and knowledge. This specific conceptualization raises a major debate, mainly about the presumption of a hierarchy from data to information to knowledge, in which the definition of each term tends to vary along certain dimensions, such as context, usefulness or interpretability.

Another perspective in defining knowledge proposes an inverse hierarchy from data to knowledge, in which knowledge can exist before information is formulated and data is measured to form information (Tuomi 1999). From this point of view, knowledge exists and, when it is articulated and formally communicated, becomes information; which then, when standardized and represented, becomes data. The main criticism of this argument lies in the fact that knowledge is embedded in its agent, and cannot exist outside of its knower (Fahey and Prusak 1998; Tuomi 1999). Thus, knowledge results from a cognitive processing triggered by the inflow of new stimuli (Alavi and Leidner 2001; Nonaka and Von Krogh 2009). Consistent with this view, it is possible to argue that information is converted to knowledge once the minds of individuals can process it and, also, knowledge becomes information once it is structured and formally represented through text, graphics, words or other symbolic forms.

Unlike the hierarchical structure of knowledge studies, whether set out in the usual direction or inversely, another research stream views knowledge as a set of information held in the individual's mind (e.g., Churchman 1972; Alavi and Leidner 2001; Malhotra 2001). As Malhotra (2001, p. 2) assumes, "knowledge resides in the user and not in the collection [of information]." Indeed, knowledge concerns information that an individual has personalized and built up according to his/her perspective with reference to facts, procedures, concepts, interpretations, ideas, observations and judgments (which might or might not be unique useful, unique, adequate, accurate and structurable). In this regard, scholars basically argue that the two concepts, knowledge and information, do not radically differ, but knowledge is the result of processing information; that is, information becomes knowledge because it is processed in the mind of an individual (Alavi and Leidner 2001). More specifically, building upon this perspective, most researchers and practitioners (Lehner 1990; Terret 1998; Gates 1999) tend to mention knowledge as synonymous with information, focusing their attention on how knowledge, as information, is effectively stored, retrieved, transferred and shared (e.g., Hendriks and Vriens 1999; Brown and Duguid 2000). Such different conceptualizations of knowledge lead to some interesting considerations. First, knowledge must be communicated in the way that makes it interpretable and accessible for anyone through being personalized. Second, a lot of information is of low value; in fact, only information adequately, actively and effectively processed in the mind of an individual can be useful, and this occurs only thanks to several deep processes such as reflection, enlightenment and learning.

Knowledge is also defined as "a fluid mix of framed experience, values, contextual information, and expert insights that provides a framework for evaluating and incorporating new experiences and information. It originates in and is applied in the minds of knowers" (Davenport and Prusak 1998, p. 5). Although this definition clearly highlights the dynamic character of knowledge (i.e., knowledge is conceived both as an outcome, that is a framework, and a process for "incorporating new experiences and information"), it does not give a clear explanation of the distinction between knowledge and information, and also fails to clarify how values and contextual information can originate and apply in the minds of individuals (Tsoukas and Vladimirou 2001). The dynamic character of knowledge also features in research by Nonaka (1991) and Nonaka and Takeuchi (1995), who state "knowledge is a dynamic human process of justifying personal belief toward the truth" (Nonaka and Takeuchi 1995, p. 58). According to these authors, when comparing knowledge to information, the latter is conceived as the "flow of messages" (p. 58), while knowledge creation occurs when messages can interact with holders' beliefs and commitments. According to Nonaka (1991), an organization is not merely an information-processing machine, but an entity that creates knowledge through such action and interaction. Hence, Nonaka and Takeuchi (1995) have identified three main characteristics that distinguish information and knowledge. First, knowledge depends on the specific perspective, intention or position of individuals, and thus, unlike information, it takes into account beliefs and commitment. Second, knowledge is always about a specific aim; i.e., it always concerns action. Third, knowledge is specifically and deeply linked to context and relationship and is therefore about meaning.

This perspective shifts the focus from an individual to a collective ontological dimension of knowledge. Knowledge can reside in the brain and body skills of the individual, or be shared among members of an organization (Lam 2000). Collective knowledge is the collective mind of an organization, because it is stored in its rules, procedures, routines, and shared norms (Walsh and Ungson 1991). Since collective knowledge exists between rather than within individuals, it can be viewed as "a 'stock' of knowledge stored as hard data, or represent knowledge in a state of flow emerging from interaction" (Lam 2000, p. 491).

Moreover, this perspective emphasizes the interplay between knowledge and action. Scholars have significantly outlined the close connection between knowledge and action, so whatever knowledge is or however it can be conceived, it is always considered able to make a difference to individuals' actions (e.g., Choo 1998; Davenport and Prusak 1998; Leonard and Sensiper 1998; Suchman 1987; Wigg 1997). In this regard, Cook and Brown (1999) distinguish "what is known" (knowledge) from "what is part of action" (knowing). Knowing "is not something that is used or necessary to action, but rather something that is a part of action. [...] Knowing is that aspect of action (or practice) that does epistemic work" (Cook and Brown 1999, p. 387). In respect of Cook and Brown (1999), Orlikowski (2002) assumes that tacit knowledge is not distinct and separable from knowing and thus from action, because it is constituted through such action. Knowing is viewed as complementing "the existing perspectives on knowledge by insisting on the essential role of human agency in accomplishing knowledgeable work" (Orlikowski 2002, p. 269). More generally, although Cook and Brown (1999) and Orlikowski (2002) view the interplay between knowledge and knowing differently, their findings move in the same direction by highlighting the contribution of social relationships to knowledge accumulation.

Building upon the different perspectives explained above, managerial literature provides a more up-to-date and comprehensive conceptualization of knowledge, clearly distinguishing it from data and information (Nonaka and Takeuchi 1995; Boisot 1995; Choo 1998; Davenport and Prusak 1998). Scholars have argued in depth about what differentiates knowledge from information and, more specifically, how knowledge requires preconditions such as values and beliefs, and is closely connected with action (Nonaka and Von Krogh 2009). Bell (1999) suggests a clear definition of these terms. Specifically, data represents a formal and ordered sequence of given items or events. Information can be conceived as an arrangement of items based on the context, showing clearly the relationships between them. Knowledge is the decisions made about the significance and meaning of events and items, which depend on specific context and/or theory. In this perspective, the definition of knowledge is developed by viewing data, information, and knowledge as three concepts that can be arranged on a single continuum, depending on human reflection, involvement and processing of the reality (Nonaka 1994; Nonaka and Von Krogh 2009).

Finally, Alavi and Leidner (2001) also identify five main perspectives in viewing knowledge: (1) a state of mind, (2) an object, (3) a process, (4) a condition of having access to information, and (5) a capability. Knowledge can be described as "a state of mind," focusing on the capacity of individuals to enrich and expand their personal knowledge through experience or study (Schubert et al. 1998). Alternatively, if knowledge is defined as "an object" (Carlsson et al. 1996; McQueen 1998; Zack 1999), the focus is mainly on seeing knowledge as a thing because it can be stored and managed in a formal way. In addition, knowledge can be viewed as a simultaneous "process" of knowing and acting (Carlsson et al. 1996; McQueen 1998; Zack 1999), where the application of expertise plays a key role (Zack 1999). In the fourth view of knowledge, i.e. as "a condition of access to information" (McQueen 1998), knowledge, especially within organizations, must be planned and managed to facilitate access. Finally, knowledge can be viewed as "a capability" with the chance to influence future action (Carlsson et al. 1996). In this case, knowledge is conceived as a capacity to use information, thanks to learning and experience, so it is not simply a capability for specific action (Watson 1999). All these summarized perspectives in interpreting knowledge lead to different decisions in terms of knowledge management within organizations. In particular, seeing knowledge as an object leads scholars to pay more attention to managing and creating stocks of knowledge, while seeing knowledge as a process focuses on flow and, in particular, on the codification and articulation of the different forms of knowledge (Carlsson et al. 1996; Alavi and Leidner 2001).

In line with previous research, this book adopts a more dynamic approach to knowledge, considering it as a fluid mix of several correlated elements, such as experience, values, contextual information and expertise. Knowledge originates and is activated in the minds of knowers (individually), as well as being rooted in organizations (collectively) because it is stored in documents, reports or organizational routines, processes, norms and practices. Knowledge as a mixture of various elements can be more or less structured, as well as codified and articulated in different ways. Knowledge is part of human agency and thus it can be seen both as a "stock" and a "process."

Thus, in what follows, I will explore organizational knowledge, focusing on the epistemological (explicit and tacit) and ontological (individual and collective) dimensions of knowledge. Then I will explore the issue of knowledge management by focusing on the processes of creation, sharing and preservation of knowledge.

1.2 Taxonomy of Knowledge

Knowledge is increasingly regarded as a crucial resource for individuals, groups, and organizations. Although people intuitively identify knowledge with individual knowledge, in recent decades corporate strategy researchers have paid more attention to the idea of organization as a body of knowledge (e.g., Nelson and Winter 1982; Grant 1996; Spender 1996a). More precisely, management theorists have viewed organization as a system that processes information and applies knowledge to solve problems, so developing new knowledge useful for further decision-making (Malhotra 2005). Organization is not merely an information-processing machine, but an entity that creates knowledge through action and interaction (Nonaka 1994). The close connection between knowledge and action is also stressed by other scholars, who recognize the dynamic character of knowledge (e.g., Weick 1991; Nonaka and Takeuchi 1995; Davenport and Prusak 1998; Cook and Brown 1999).

As Nonaka and Takeuchi (1995, pp. 58–59) stated, "information is a flow of messages, while knowledge is created by that very flow of information, anchored in the beliefs and commitment of its holder. This understanding emphasizes that knowledge is essentially related to human action." Davenport and Prusak (1998, p. 5) assume that knowledge can also be rooted in organization because it is "embedded not only in documents or repositories but also in organizational routines, processes, practices, and norms."

According to Weick (1991), what people know can be turned into organizational knowledge only if translated into a set of activities. Organization is a "collective mind […] a distinct higher-order pattern of interrelated activities" embedded in and generated by individual and group actions (Weick and Roberts 1993, p. 374). Similarly, Cook and Brown (1999) distinguish the epistemology of possession (knowledge) from the epistemology of practice as action (knowing) and stress the interplay between them. They assume that individual and group knowledge is mainly expressed through what people do, and that human and organizational actions generate a process of knowing that additionally enriches organizational knowledge. In this regard, they conclude that knowledge and knowing are not competing but complementary and mutually enabling.

Since defining organizational knowledge is very hard, so much so that it finds very little consensus in the literature, this paragraph aims to investigate "what constitutes it," rather than "what it is." Organizational knowledge is analyzed along two dimensions: epistemological and ontological (e.g., Cook and Brown 1999; Lam 2000). The former dimension concerns the modes of expression of knowledge, such as explicit and tacit, while the latter relates to the locus of knowledge that resides at individual and collective level (Lam 2000). The distinction between tacit and explicit forms of knowledge (the epistemological dimension) and individual and collective forms of knowledge (the ontological dimension) will be explored in the next paragraphs.

1.2.1 Explicit and Tacit Forms of Knowledge

Management scientists and practitioners have often paid more attention to explicit than tacit knowledge, because of the assumption of legitimacy generated by the ability to record explicit knowledge (Jordan and Jones 1997). Tacit knowledge has been frequently treated as an informal and obscure matter that needs to be translated into explicit knowledge if it is to be understood and used, or an inchoate and hidden subject inaccessible for practical purposes (Alavi and Leidner 2001). Polanyi (1966) defines tacit knowledge as something everyone knows but cannot describe. Tacit and explicit knowledge are not variants of each other, but are two distinct forms of knowledge that cannot be mistaken for or changed into one other. In order to explain the difference between explicit and tacit knowledge, Polanyi (1967) gives the example of the bicycle, asserting that: people are able to ride a bicycle if they know how to stay upright and to turn the handlebars to prevent a fall. Explicit knowledge of how to ride may help you to improve this ability, but you need tacit knowledge to stay upright. In this regard, each form of knowledge has its own path and purpose and may help to improve the other, but no one form can be converted into the other (Cook and Brown 1999).

More specifically, tacit knowledge is made up of cognitive and technical elements. The cognitive component consists of mental maps, beliefs, values and paradigms, while the technical aspects concern the practical skills and abilities needed for a particular job (Nonaka 1994). On the other hand, explicit knowledge is codified and communicated by symbolic and natural language, and appears valuable (Nonaka 1994). It tries to avoid the risk of rigidity and inflexibility of formalization, which could harm organizational performance (Alavi and Leidner 2001). For instance, choosing soft or hard-sell tactics to approach customers represents tacit knowledge, while the manual of instruction that sellers use with clients to explain the correct functioning of a product constitutes explicit knowledge (Alavi and Leidner 2001).

Explicit knowledge has been also considered as the third phase of personalization of information, after the collection of objective data (facts and numbers) and their interpretation. Tacit knowledge, on the other hand, can represent the process of applying expertise, and the capability to influence action. In this regard, the tacit dimension of knowledge may be always associated with the perspective of "state of mind," which views knowledge as the state of knowing and understanding (Alavi and Leidner 2001). This different perspective on knowledge influences the identification of specific knowledge management systems in regard to tacit and explicit forms of knowledge, overcoming the original lack of study of interrelationships among the various type of knowledge (Spender 1996b; Nonaka 1994). Thus, explicit knowledge may be associated with systems which help absorb, store and transfer relevant information. Tacit knowledge, however, may be developed through access to the sources of knowledge, rather than to the information itself, to stimulate a broader and deeper implicit assimilation of knowledge flows, and to increase individual and organizational competencies (Alavi and Leidner 2001).

Indeed, tacit knowledge may not be considered an ephemeral set of hidden information, unusable in practice, but, on the contrary, as an intuitive way to respond to an unconscious interpretation of the complex pattern of things, without being able to identify specifically what characteristics of the situation are guiding your mind and body (Polanyi 1967). Explicit knowledge starts from the rational formalization of interpreted data and tries to bring about better performance through an intellectual rather than a practical approach (Polanyi 1967). Tacit knowledge represents procedural (know-how), conditional (know-when) and pragmatic (useful) knowledge for individuals, groups and organizations. Unlike tacit knowledge, explicit knowledge constitutes declarative (know about), causal (know why), and relational or interactional (know with) knowledge among relevant variables in informational settings (Alavi and Leidner 2001).

1.2.2 Individual and Collective Forms of Knowledge

Besides investigating the epistemological dimension of knowledge, some research has looked at the ontological dimension, aiming to understand the processes of creation, sharing and storage of knowledge at individual and collective level, as well as the interplay among them (Lam 2000). Up to now, individual and collective taxonomy of knowledge has been adopted, with almost the same meaning from the start, in spite of the broader and deeply significant development in methods of interpretation of tacit and explicit knowledge (Alavi and Leidner 2001). In particular, individual knowledge concerns types of knowledge created by and inherent in the individual, while collective knowledge (also known as social knowledge) is knowledge created by and inherent in the collective actions of a group (Alavi and Leidner 2001).

In respect of tacit and explicit knowledge, which are considered to be two distinct forms of knowledge because we do not need to explain how one works in terms of the other, individual knowledge may be able to influence organizational knowledge only if converted into collective knowledge by using institutional and social mechanisms (Walsh and Ungson 1991). This assumption is far from recent. In the past, Penrose (1959) and Arrow (1962) have already underlined the role of learning through developing strategies and coordination to convert individual knowledge into organizational growth. Similarly, Weber (1980) suggests the use of bureaucratic procedures and control to transfer individual knowledge to the organizational level. More generally, the possibility of transferring individual knowledge into collective knowledge without obstacles has always been acknowledged (Huber 1991). Taking an anthropomorphic perspective on knowledge, such scholars view the organization as a human entity with human-like biological functioning and capabilities of mind, memory, consciousness and feelings.

The anthropomorphic view of knowledge has received some criticism over time. Some scholars hold that learning in organizations is individual rather than collective (Simon 1991), and that individual knowledge is what brings about change in organizations (Cohen and Sproull 1991). Other doubts about the anthropomorphic perspective concern the feasibility of articulating and storing knowledge at the organizational level, so supporting the significant and exclusive role of individual behaviors (e.g., Allport 1924; Argyris and Schon 1978; Sandelands and Stablein 1987).

A different way to view the organization is inspired by Durkheim's (1964) notion of the "conscience collective." Building upon Durkheim's (1964) research, some scholars have begun to see organization as a social context, rather than a biological entity, in which collective knowledge is activated by a set of interactions between individuals within the boundaries given by the organization's designers (Sandelands and Stablein 1987). Collective knowledge is considered as a system of collective practices selected and transferred within organizational boundaries (Sandelands and Stablein 1987). This assumption has created the conditions for research on knowledge creation and sharing in communities of practice (e.g., Wasko and Faraj 2005). Communities of practice are recognized as a way to transfer collective knowledge within and outside of organizational settings, so becoming a powerful source of knowledge management and competitive advantage (Spender 1994).

Other scholars highlight the concept of collective knowledge by distinguishing it from group knowledge. In particular, Weick and Roberts (1993) state that collective knowledge, i.e. the collective mind, is the result of individual isolation absorbed by group inclusiveness, which allows influence, control and participation by group members. Also, a group may exist without a collective mind, and a collective mind may occur without forming a group, as a system of mindful practices generated by interactions among individuals within or outside of a group. Organizational forms which inhibit the formation of a collective mind may not develop a high degree of reliability (Bierly and Spender 1994).

Similarly, Nelson and Winter (1982) also suggest that collective knowledge is different from group knowledge because it is embedded in institutionalized practices, expressed by organizational routines and operating procedures. Group knowledge is the sum of previous individual knowledge, and is represented by explicit analysis. On the contrary, collective knowledge emerges after individuals begin to engage in practices within a context of interaction. It becomes only partly evident through carrying out practices arising from the history and evolution of the organizational activity (Polanyi 1967).

1.3 Managing Knowledge

The management and processing of knowledge are considered to be the most important source of a firm's renewable and sustainable competitive advantage (e.g., Nonaka 1994; Prahalad and Hamel 1994; Nonaka and Takeuchi 1995; Martinez 2011). Often organizations possess knowledge, but are not able to exploit it. Organizational knowledge creation and sharing have long been under investigation by a number of scholars from different countries and disciplines because these processes are acknowledged as critical to knowledge management (e.g., Alavi and Leidner 2001). Sometimes, instead, knowledge is not accessible because the organization cannot store it. Some scholars have decided to address their research to knowledge preservation, rather than knowledge creation and sharing, because they see it as crucial for knowledge advancement (e.g., Romhardt 1997; Probst 1998; Probst et al. 2006; Alavi and Leidner 2001; Lazaric et al. 2003; Davidavičienė and Raudeliūnienė 2010; Maina 2012). More generally, as Gold and Arvind Malhotra (2001, p. 186) state, "organizations may not be equally predisposed for successful launch and maintenance of knowledge management initiatives."

Knowledge management is a process that enables organizations to identify, capture and effectively leverage collective knowledge in an organization (Von Krough 1999). It consists of various sets of socially enacted "knowledge processes," such as knowledge creation (known as contraction or development), knowledge sharing (known as transfer, distribution or dissemination), and knowledge preservation (known as storage and retrieval). In truth, besides those just listed, scholars have also identified other stages considered crucial for knowledge management, such as knowledge identification, knowledge application (known as use or exploitation), etc. (e.g., Probst 1998; Alavi and Leidner 2001; Gold and Arvind Malhotra 2001; Probst et al. 2006). For instance, Probst et al. (2006) state that knowledge management consists of coordinated frameworks, such as knowledge goals, identification, acquirement, development, distribution, use, preservation and audit. However, using a more inclusive meaning, the processes of creation, sharing and preservation of knowledge already take these phases into account, for example by identification and application, and, thus, may explain knowledge management in an organization. Moreover, the success of an organization does not arise from a detailed identification of the various phases that constitute knowledge management, but from analysis of the mechanisms and tools enabling the management and processing of such knowledge.

The next paragraphs will focus on the processes of creation, sharing and preservation of organizational knowledge, distinguishing between mechanisms and tools enacting such processes in organizations.

1.4 Knowledge Creation and Sharing

Knowledge creation and sharing are important processes of knowledge management in organizational settings (e.g., Nonaka and Takeuchi 1995; Alavi and Leidner 2001; Nonaka and Toyama 2002; Nonaka et al. 2006; Pezzillo Iacono et al. 2012). Knowledge management refers to identifying and leveraging collective knowledge in an organization to improve the firm's competitiveness (Von Krogh 1999).

Nonaka et al. (2006, p. 1179) define organizational knowledge creation as "the process of making available and amplifying knowledge created by individuals as well as crystallizing and connecting it with an organization's knowledge system."

Therefore, organizational knowledge creation is a process whereby knowledge is transformed from an individual to a collective state (Nonaka and Takeuchi 1995) through dynamic interactions among individuals, the organization and the environment (Nonaka and Toyama 2002). This transformation occurs in a dynamic process involving various organizational levels, where "distinctive individual knowledge is exchanged, evaluated, and integrated with that of others in the organization" (Boland and Tenkasi 1995, p. 358).

The link between the individual level, where knowledge resides, and the organizational level, where knowledge is converted into economic and competitive value for the firm, is the knowledge-sharing process (Hendriks 1999). Through knowledge sharing, knowledge is made available to others. In particular, "knowledge held by an individual is converted into a form that can be understood, absorbed, and used by other individuals" (Ipe 2003, p. 341). Knowledge sharing is a voluntary act (Davenport 1997) that implies a relationship between at least two individuals: one that possesses the knowledge and the other that acquires the knowledge (Hendriks 1999).

In what follows, this study will stress the processes of knowledge creation and sharing and the mechanisms and tools enabling them to take place in organizations.

1.4.1 The Processes of Knowledge Creation and Sharing

Nonaka (1994) develops the concept of a spiral of knowledge creation to show how knowledge is created and shared in organizational settings through social interactions and collaborative processes. In this model, knowledge moves upward in an organization, starting at the individual level, moving to the group level, and then up to the firm level, involving a continual interplay between the tacit and explicit dimensions of knowledge (Inkpen and Dinur 1998). Nonaka's research (Nonaka 1994; Nonaka and Takeuchi 1995; Nonaka et al. 2000; Nonaka and Toyama 2003) identifies four processes of knowledge creation (known as the SECI model): socialization, externalization, combination, and internalization. Figure 1.1 shows Nonaka's SECI model (1994).

Socialization is the process of converting tacit knowledge to new tacit knowledge through shared experiences and social interaction (Nonaka et al. 2000). Externalization refers to converting tacit knowledge into explicit knowledge, so that it can be shared by others to become the basis of new knowledge (Nonaka et al. 2000; Nonaka and Toyama 2003). Through the combination process, new explicit knowledge is created by merging, categorizing, reclassifying and synthesizing existing explicit knowledge. Internalization refers to the conversion of the explicit knowledge created and shared into new tacit knowledge, through applying it in practical situations and making it the base for new routines (Nonaka et al. 2000; Nonaka and Toyama 2003). These four processes are highly interdependent and intertwined, highlighting the coexistence of the two types of knowledge, tacit and explicit, interacting continuously. Moreover, through this knowledge-creating

Fig. 1.1 SECI model of
knowledge creation. *Source*
Nonaka et al. (2000)

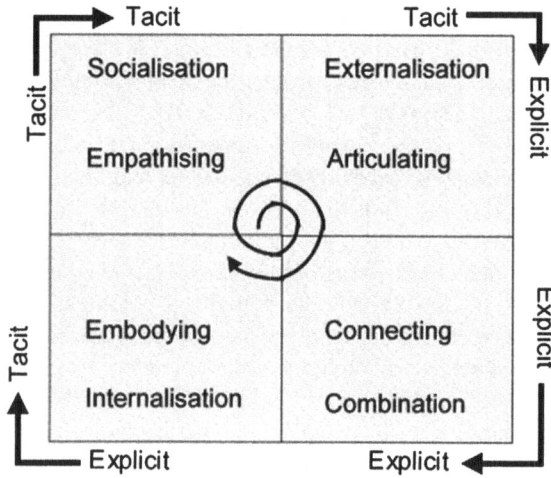

process, personal subjective knowledge is validated, connected to and synthesized with others' knowledge (Nonaka and Takeuchi 1995).

Nonaka and Toyama (2003) show that the knowledge-creating process is context-specific in terms of time, space, and relationship with others. In other words, knowledge needs a place where information is given meaning through interpretation to become knowledge, and this context is recognized in the concept of "ba" (Nonaka and Konno 1998). Ba is "an existential place where participants share their contexts and create new meanings through interactions. Participants of ba bring in their own contexts, and through interactions with others and the environment, the contexts of ba, participants, and the environment change" (Nonaka and Toyama 2003, p. 7). Ba can be a physical, virtual or mental space, where knowledge is acquired through individual experiences, or reflections on others' experience (Nonaka et al. 2006).

Nonaka and Konno (1998) identify four types of ba for creating knowledge: originating ba, interacting ba, cyber ba and exercising ba. In originating ba, the process of organizational knowledge creation begins, representing socialization among individuals. Originating ba is a place in which individuals interact face-to-face, sharing emotions, feelings, experiences and mental models. Interacting ba supports externalization, which is a space where tacit knowledge is converted to explicit knowledge and shared among individuals through work with peers, dialog and collaboration. Cyber ba refers to a virtual place of interaction, where new explicit knowledge is created through a process of combination. Finally, the exercising ba involves the conversion of explicit to tacit knowledge through the process of internalization. In this space, training from instructors and colleagues and repetitive exercises support continuous individual learning.

Understanding the characteristics of various types of ba and of the stages of knowledge creation is important for enhancing organizational knowledge creation (Alavi and Leidner 2001) and for identifying the most effective mechanisms and/or tools for knowledge creation and sharing (e.g., Nonaka and Toyama 2003; Panahi et al. 2013).

1.4.2   Mechanisms and Tools for Knowledge Creation and Sharing

Hendriks (1999) has shown that knowledge creation and sharing is based on the relationship between at least two parties: one that possesses knowledge and the other that acquires knowledge. In this relationship, the first party should communicate its knowledge using an appropriate knowledge transfer tool, while the other party should be able to perceive these expressions of knowledge and make sense of them (Hendriks 1999). Knowledge can take different forms, for example in actions, in speech or in writing, as well as in the perception of the knowledge; and sense-making can take place by, for example, watching others perform tasks or actions, by listening, or by reading books (Hendriks 1999).

Therefore, there are several mechanisms and tools that can support the processes of knowledge creation and sharing. Holtham and Courtney (1998) classify the mechanisms as follows: informal or formal, and personal or impersonal. For instance, informal mechanisms, such as informal discussions or coffee-break conversations, are effective in promoting socialization, but can preclude wider dissemination. Formal mechanisms, such as plant tours, training sessions, etc., can encourage dissemination but may inhibit creativity. Formal transfer mechanisms appear to be more effective than informal mechanisms, although they inhibit creativity and innovation (Alavi and Leidner 2001). Furthermore, personal mechanisms, such as apprenticeships, are a formal and personal channel of knowledge transfer. Such mechanisms are more effective for sharing highly context-specific knowledge. Impersonal channels, such as knowledge repositories, allow individuals and groups to generalize and thus transfer knowledge across organizational boundaries. More generally, the most effective transfer mechanisms depend upon the type of knowledge being transferred (Inkpen and Dinur 1998).

Nonaka and Toyama (2003) also identify certain mechanisms and/or tools for knowledge creation and sharing within the model of knowledge creation (i.e., SECI). In the socialization process, the articulation of tacit knowledge into new tacit knowledge can take place where people spend time together or live in the same environment, typically through a traditional apprenticeship. In such cases, the conversion of tacit knowledge into explicit knowledge such as concepts, images, and written documents is based on dialog. This mechanism allows people to articulate and share tacit knowledge with each other. Some tools, such as computerized communication networks and databases, can facilitate the combination process whereby new explicit knowledge is created. Within the internalization process, the conversion of explicit knowledge into new tacit knowledge can be supported by training programs or by reading documents or manuals. Through these tools, individuals can internalize the explicit knowledge written in such documents to enrich their tacit knowledge base.

More generally, information technology (IT) has been regarded as one of the main enablers of knowledge creation and sharing (e.g., Martinez 2004; Hendriks 1999; Alavi and Leidner 2001; Sher and Lee 2004; Skok and Kalmanovitch 2005; Pezzillo Iacono et al. 2012). Alavi and Leidner (2001) propose a review of the role of IT in supporting knowledge creation and sharing processes in organizations, identifying three common applications. These are: the coding and sharing of best practices; the creation of corporate knowledge directories; and the creation of knowledge networks. The first application is internal benchmarking with the aim of transferring best practices (O'Dell and Grayson 1998). The creation of corporate knowledge directories is the mapping of internal expertise, so as to rapidly locate an individual who has the knowledge needed to solve a problem. Face-to-face and IT-assisted tools, such as knowledge networks, computer networks, discussion groups, online forums and virtual communities for communication and discussion, support the creation, sharing and generation of new beliefs and ideas (Henderson et al. 1997; Martinez 2004). Using these tools, an individual can post a question, such as "does anybody know" or "request help" from the discussion group. Moreover, Alavi and Leidner (2001) also provide a set of IT tools for supporting knowledge management processes in organizations. For instance, email and group support systems encourage more interactions between individuals, supporting collaboration, coordination and communication and, consequently, the growth of knowledge creation (Nonaka 1994). Other examples are intranets that provide access to a multitude of organizational information, and intelligent agent software that allows the development of interest profiles of organizational members in order to identify whoever would be an appropriate recipient of point-to-point electronic messages exchanged among other members (O'Dell and Grayson 1998).

Building upon previous research (e.g., Nonaka 1994; Nonaka and Takeuchi 1995; Marwick 2001), Panahi et al. (2013) summarize the main mechanisms and tools, both face-to-face and IT-assisted, enabling knowledge creation and sharing within the SECI model of Nonaka (1994). Table 1.1 shows the mechanisms and tools enabling the processes of knowledge creation and sharing within organizations.

Table 1.1 Mechanisms and tools for knowledge creating and sharing

IT-assisted		Face to face	
Socialization (*tacit to tacit*)	*Socialization* (*tacit to tacit*)	*Externalization* (*tacit to explicit*)	*Externalization* (*tacit to explicit*)
– Online real-time meetings – Synchronous communication (Chat) – Online community of practice – Groupware systems – Social media	– Team meetings – Discussions – Interpersonal interactions – Apprenticeship – Participation – Observation	– Dialog with team – Answering questions – Story-telling – Metaphors/analogies	– Answering questions – Annotations – Blogs/Wikis – Discussion forums – Collaborative systems – Groupware systems – Phone/video conferencing
Combination (*explicit to explicit*)	*Combination* (*explicit to explicit*)	*Internalization* (*explicit to tacit*)	*Internalization* (*explicit to tacit*)
– All forms of technologies – Text search – Document categorization – Podcast/vodcast – Blogs/wikis – RSS – Mashups	– Books – Papers – Reports – Presentations – Indexes, etc.	– Learning by doing – Learning from books, reports, presentations, lectures, etc.	– Visualization – Video/audio presentations – Online learning – E-mail – Webpage

Source adapted from Panahi et al. (2013)

1.5 Knowledge Preservation

Knowledge preservation has been recognized as one of the crucial steps in managing and processing knowledge in organizations (e.g., Romhardt 1997; Probst 1998; Probst et al. 2006; Alavi and Leidner 2001; Lazaric et al. 2003; Davidavičienė and Raudeliūnienė 2010; Maina 2012). How to avoid losing knowledge is one of the biggest everyday challenges for organizations and managers. In fact, empirical evidence shows that while organizations create knowledge and learn, they also forget (e.g., Darr et al. 1995; Schiavone and Agrifoglio 2012). Thus, "the storage, organization, and retrieval of organizational knowledge, also referred to as organizational memory […], constitute an important aspect of effective organizational knowledge management" (Alavi and Leidner 2001, p. 118). Once knowledge is lost, managers can only replace it through high investment in developing new knowledge and/or in acquiring it from outside the organization. Building upon research by Romhardt (1997) and Probst et al. (2006), Davidavičienė

Table 1.2 Main causes of knowledge loss

		Individual	Collective	Electronic
Deleted memory		Termination death amnesia retirement	Dissolving of adjusted teams reengineering outsourcing of competencies	Irreversible data loss viruses hardware mistakes system crash insufficient backup hackers
Access	Limited	Overload/limited transfers illness vacation/inadequate training service according to regulation	Making taboo of routines Collective sabotage	Reversible data loss overload/limited interface problems
	Permanent	Overload/permanent No awareness of the importance of own knowledge Inner termination	Sale of company division migration of teams cover-up	Permanent incompatibility of systems Overload/permanent wrong codification

Source Davidavičienė and Raudeliūnienė (2010, p. 824)

and Raudeliūnienė (2010) provide a detailed list of causes of knowledge loss in organizations at the individual, collective and electronic level. Table 1.2 shows the main causes of knowledge loss in an organization.

Having clarified the crucial role of knowledge preservation in knowledge management, it would be useful to explain what knowledge preservation is.

Researchers have linked the concept of knowledge preservation to organizational memory (Probst and Romhardt 1997; Romhardt 1997; Probst 1998; Alavi and Leidner 2001; Davidavičienė and Raudeliūnienė 2010). According to these authors, knowledge preservation refers to organizational/corporate memory, which consists of explicit and tacit knowledge residing in various component forms, such as written documents, knowledge management systems, databases, organizational procedures, norms, acquired by individuals and networks of individuals (Alavi and Leidner 2001). Organizational memory, and thus the process of knowledge preservation, aids workers "in reapplying workable solutions in the form of standards and procedures, which in turn avoid the waste of organizational resources in replicating previous work" (Alavi and Leidner 2001, p. 118). On the other hand, it can have a negative influence on a firm's performance because of reproducing organizational routines and procedures that lead individuals to maintain the status quo and thus increase their resistance to change (Alavi and Leidner 2001).

These studies have paid more attention to the processes and tools enabling organizations to preserve organizational knowledge than to the issue of conceptualization. However, sometimes the analysis of processes enables scholars to further conceptualize knowledge preservation. In this regard, knowledge preservation is widely recognized as the process of selection, storage and effective actualization of organizational knowledge (Romhardt 1997; Probst 1998; Probst et al. 2006; Davidavičienė and Raudeliūnienė 2010) or, similarly, as the process enabling workers to store, organize and retrieve knowledge in organizations (Alavi and Leidner 2001).

The following section will highlight the process of knowledge preservation and the mechanisms and tools enabling organizations to preserve such knowledge.

1.5.1 The Process of Knowledge Preservation

After organizational knowledge has been developed or acquired from the outside, it must be carefully preserved. As explained above, a large part of the literature agrees that preserving knowledge is the process of enabling organizations to select, store and effectively actualize knowledge which has already been acquired or developed (e.g., Probst and Romhardt 1997; Romhardt 1997; Probst 1998; Alavi and Leidner 2001; Probst et al. 2006; Davidavičienė and Raudeliūnienė 2010).

Romhardt (1997) states that organizations which aim to develop new knowledge have to master three basic stages (or processes) of knowledge management: selection, storage, and actualization. These phases, known as the three main stages of knowledge preservation, form the basis for further investigations (e.g., Probst 1998; Probst et al. 2006; Davidavičienė and Raudeliūnienė 2010).

Selection concerns the identification of organizational knowledge that may be useful in the future and therefore should be protected (Romhardt 1997). Organizations cannot preserve all the information available to them. Among all the data on offer to them, they should select only those that are worth preserving. This assumption is elaborated by Probst (1998, p. 27), who states that: organizations should identify "core areas of their organizational knowledge base and establish a pragmatic selection stage for knowledge to be saved. The guiding rule should be to preserve only information that will be usable for a third party in the future." Since this stage is difficult and expensive, firms cannot and should not keep everything, but select items of knowledge that are worth protecting. Thus, firms aim to "transfer valuable data, information and skills into organizational systems in which they can be used by the whole company" (Romhardt 1997, n.p.).

The second stage of knowledge preservation is storage. This stage enables individuals to save the organizational knowledge base in a suitable form (Romhardt 1997). After selecting the knowledge that is worth protecting, the organization must effectively store it. Romhardt (1997) identifies three forms of storage of organizational knowledge: individual, collective and electronic. The first enables organizations to avoid the permanent loss of valuable knowledge possessed by individuals. Lay-off, termination, retirement or death are some of the most frequent causes of individual knowledge loss (see Table 1.2 for more details). When one of these occurs, individual knowledge that has not been preserved previously will no longer be available in the future. Social and material incentives, exit barriers, organizational climate and training are some of the mechanisms that allow organizations to preserve individual knowledge (Romhardt 1997; Alavi and Leidner 2001). Collective storage, on the other hand, aims to save knowledge into the collective memory of an organization. Collective memory is deeply rooted in an organization and is stored by means of the social and cognitive relationships that workers establish (Romhardt 1997). Finally, storage in electronic memory emphasizes the multiple electronic storage capabilities of IT systems, rather than traditional tools (Romhardt 1997; Davidavičienė and Raudeliūnienė 2010). As Davidavičienė and Raudeliūnienė (2010) remark, a high level of ICT usage increases interaction and exchange of information among workers, as well as providing many possible ways to preserve knowledge.

Finally, the last stage of knowledge preservation is the actualization of previously stored organizational knowledge. As Romhardt (1997) suggests, knowledge preservation does not conclude with the storage of organizational knowledge, but in making such knowledge available in acceptable quality for decision-making. Knowledge preservation is a continual and systematic process. Outdated storage systems and the storing of incorrect information could lead managers to make wrong decisions, so causing more damage to organizational performance. Therefore, organizations should pay more attention to the actualization stage of knowledge preservation and, in particular, to "trust" in data quality and "access" to information. Indeed, as Romhardt (1997, n.p.) remarks, "if trust in data quality exists and easy access to the system can be guaranteed, systems will be fed and will be used in ways that increase data quality. If the actual database is already full of mistakes, trust cannot be built and no-one will invest much energy into the system. Data quality decreases further and the system dies. In times of short half-life death may arrive very quickly."

1.5.2 Mechanisms and Tools for Preserving Knowledge

As with knowledge creation and sharing, there are certain mechanisms and tools that enable organizations to select, store and actualize knowledge. Managerial literature mainly focuses on the process of knowledge preservation, with the aim of understanding how organizational knowledge can and should be effectively preserved, while IS literature pays more attention to the tools—traditional or IT-assisted—for preserving such knowledge. By contrast, the mechanisms enabling the preservation of organizational knowledge have not been deeply explored. Indeed, while the knowledge preservation process has been clearly explained, there is no clear distinction between the mechanisms and tools enabling organizations to select, store and actualize the different forms of knowledge. The literature mainly addresses the issues of how and where organizational knowledge is preserved, while the question of how to preserve it deserves further study.

Building upon previous literature (e.g., Romhardt 1997; Alavi and Leidner 2001; Davidavičienė and Raudeliūnienė 2010), this paragraph will try to shed light on the mechanisms and tools enabling individuals to preserve different forms of knowledge in organizations.

In order to explain knowledge preservation, and in particular the storage stage, Romhardt (1997) and Alavi and Leidner (2001) distinguish individual memory from collective (known as organizational) memory and identify some mechanisms and tools enabling organizations to preserve individual and collective forms of knowledge. With reference to individual memory preservation, Romhardt (1997, n.p.) assumes that "the easiest way to save intellectual capital is to create an atmosphere that does not stimulate thoughts of changing companies. [...] If we think that an excellent working atmosphere added to an average income, is sufficient for the long-term commitment of an employee, we will most probably lose some of our best experts. Exit barriers may be created by social or material incentive systems. [...] The establishment of flexible cooperation with these alumni is a rewarding option to preserve the access to their know-how after the termination of their contract. Alternative forms of cooperation are operations as trainers, consultants and selective cooperation in difficult talks with old customers and more." This leads us to deduce that the organizational climate, social and monetary incentives, and cooperation are some of the mechanisms that enable the preservation of individual forms of knowledge in organizations. With reference to collective memory preservation, Romhardt (1997) assumes that the storage of collective memory is drawn from the individuals' capability to root their past experiences in the organization. The author also identifies some tools useful for storing such experiences, such as written documents (minutes, manuals, etc.), shared spoken language (vocabulary), and social interaction (workshops, meetings, teamwork, etc.) In this regard, it leads us toward a logical conclusion that the mechanisms enabling individuals to preserve knowledge seem to be written, verbal and physical communication and, though little emphasized, the social context.

Like Romhardt (1997), Alavi and Leidner (2001) also explore the mechanisms and tools enabling individuals to store and retrieve individual and collective memory in organizations. In particular, they assume that individual memory is "developed based on a person's observations, experiences, and actions," while collective memory "extends beyond the individual's memory to include other components such as organizational culture, transformations (production processes and work procedures), structure (formal organizational roles), ecology (physical work setting) and information archives (both internal and external to the organization)" (Alavi and Leidner 2001, p. 118). Like Romhardt (1997), they do not distinguish between mechanisms and tools enabling organizations to preserve knowledge, but provide some new interesting insights on the link between structural elements in the organization—routines, norms, procedures, shared norms, artifacts and vocabulary—and knowledge preservation. Organizational structure helps "in storing and reapplying workable solutions in the form of standards and procedures, which in turn avoid the waste of organizational resources in replicating previous work" (Alavi and Leidner 2001, p. 118). However, as I will explain later, structure is not only a medium for performing actions in organizations, but also the outcome of reproducing such actions.

Finally, building upon the previous research of Romhardt (1997) and Probst and Romhardt (1997), Davidavičienė and Raudeliūnienė (2010) classify IT-assisted

Table 1.3 IT-assisted tools in the stages of preserving knowledge

KPP	Km systems	ICT tools
Select	Discovery systems	Databases, web based access to data, data mining, web portals, best practices and lessons learned databases, video conferencing, electronic discussion group, e-mai
Store and actualize	Capture systems	Expert systems, chat groups, best practices and lessons learned databases, computer based communication, and computer based simulation
	Sharing systems	Team collaboration tools, web based access to data, best practice databases, lessons learned systems, expertise locator systems
Apply	Application systems	Troubleshooting systems, case-based reasoning systems, decision support systems, expert systems, enterprise resource planning systems, management information systems

Source Davidavičienė and Raudeliūnienė (2010, p. 825)

tools used at different stages of knowledge preservation. As suggested by Alavi and Leidner (2001), in comparison to traditional tools, IT-assisted tools can be effective in enhancing organizational memory, since they increase the speed at which organizational memory can be accessed. Table 1.3 shows the IT-assisted tools that enable individuals to select, store and effectively actualize knowledge in organizations.

References

Alavi, M., & Leidner, D. E. (2001). Review: Knowledge management and knowledge management systems: Conceptual foundations and research issues. *MIS Quarterly*, 107–136.

Allport, F. H. (1924). *Social psychology*. Boston: Houghton Mifflin.

Argyris, C., & Schon, D. A. (1978). *Organizational learning: A theory of action perspective*. Reading: Addison-Wesley.

Arrow, K. (1962). The economic implications of learning by doing. *Review of Economic Studies, 29*, 155–173.

Bell, M. (1979). The exploitation of indigenous knowledge or the indigenous exploitation of knowledge: Whose use of what for what? *The IDS Bullettin, 10*(2), 44–50.

Bell, D. (1999). *The axial age of technology foreword: 1999*. In *The coming of the post-industrial society*. New York: Basic Books (Special Anniversary Edition).

Bierly, P. E., & Spender, J. C. (1994). The culture of high reliability organizations: The case of the nuclear submarine. *Journal of Management, 21*(4), 639–656.

Boisot, M. H. (1995). *Information space: A framework for learning in organizations, institutions and culture*. London: Routledge.

Boland, R. J, Jr, & Tenkasi, R. V. (1995). Perspective making and perspective taking in communities of knowing. *Organization Science, 6*(4), 350–372.

Brown, J. S., & Duguid, P. (2000). Mysteries of the region: Knowledge dynamics in silicon valley. *The Silicon Valley Edge*, 16–45.

Carlsson, S. A., El Sawy, O. A., Eriksson, I, Raven, A. (1996). Gaining competitive advantage through shared knowledge creation: In search of a new design theory for strategic information systems. In *Proceedings of the Fourth European Conference on Information Systems* (pp. 1067–1075), Lisbon, July 2–4.

Choo, C. W. (1998). *The knowing organization: How organizations use information to construct meaning, create knowledge, and make decisions*. New York: Oxford University Press.

Churchman, C. W. (1972). *The design of inquiring systems: Basic concepts of systems and organization*. New York: Bencis Books.

Cohen, M. D., & Sproull, L. S. (Eds.), (1991). Introduction to the special issue on organizational learning. *Organization Science, 2*(1), unnumbered.

Cook, S. D. N., & Brown, J. S. (1999). Bridging epistemologies: The generative dance between organizational knowledge and organizational knowing. *Organization Science, 10*(4), 381–400.

Darr, E. D., Argote, L., & Epple, D. (1995). The acquisition, transfer and depreciation of knowledge in service organizations: Productivity in franchises. *Management Science, 41*(11), 1750–1762.

Davenport, T. H. (1997). *Information ecology*. Oxford: Oxford University Press.

Davenport, T. H., & Prusak, L. (1998). *Working knowledge*. Boston: Harvard Business School Press.

Davidavičienė, V., & Raudeliūnienė, J. (2010). ICT in tacit knowledge preservation. In *The 6th International Scientific Conference "Business and Management 2010"* (pp. 822–828), Selected Papers, (2), 13–14 May 2010, Vilnius.

Dretske, F. (1981). *Knowledge and the flow of information*. Cambridge: MIT Press.

Durkheim, E. (1964). *The rules of sociological method*. New York: Free Press.

Fahey, L., & Prusak, L. (1998). The eleven deadliest sins of knowledge management. *California Management Review, 40*(3), 265.

Gates, B. (1999). *Business @ the speed of thought*. London: Penguin Books.

Gold, A. H., & Arvind Malhotra, A. H. S. (2001). Knowledge management: An organizational capabilities perspective. *Journal of Management Information Systems, 18*(1), 185–214.

Grant, R. M. (1996). Toward a knowledge-based theory of the firm. *Strategic Management Journal, 17*(2), 109–122.

Hamel, G., & Prahalad, C. K. (1990). The core competence of the corporation. *Harvard Business Review, 68*(3), 79–81.

Henderson, J. C., Sussman, S. W., & Thomas, J. B. (1997). Creating and exploiting knowledge for fast-cycle organizational response: The center for army lessons learned. *Advances in Applied Business Strategy, 5*(4), 103–128.

Hendriks, P. (1999). Why share knowledge? The influence of ICT on the motivation for knowledge sharing. *Knowledge and Process Management, 6*(2), 91–100.

Hendriks, P. H. J., & Vriens, D. J. (1999). Knowledge-based systems and knowledge management: Friends or foes? *Information & Management, 35*, 113–125.

Holtham, C., & Courtney, N. (1998). *The executive learning ladder: A knowledge creation process grounded in the strategic information systems domain*. In AMCIS 1998 Proceedings, Baltimore, August, pp. 594–597.

Huber, G. (1991). Organizational learning: The contributing processes and the literatures. *Organization Science, 2*(1), 88–115.

Inkpen, A., & Dinur, I. (1998). Knowledge management processes and international joint ventures. *Organization Science, 9*(4), 454–468.

Ipe, M. (2003). Knowledge sharing in organizations: A conceptual framework. *Human Resource Development Review, 2*(4), 337–359.

Jordan, J., & Jones, P. (1997). Assessing your company's knowledge management style. *Long Range Planning, 30*(3), 392–398.

Lam, A. (2000). Tacit knowledge, organizational learning and societal institutions: An integrated framework. *Organization Studies, 21*(3), 487–513.

Lazaric, N., Mangolte, P. A., & Massué, M. L. (2003). Articulation and codification of collective know-how in the steel industry: evidence from blast furnace control in France. *Research Policy, 32*(10), 1829–1847.

Lehner, F. (1990). Expert systems for organizational and managerial tasks. *Information & Management, 23*(1), 31–41.

Leonard, D., & Sensiper, S. (1998). The role of tacit knowledge in group innovation. *California Management Review, 40*(3), 112–132.

Leonard-Barton, D. (1992). Core capabilities and core rigidities: A paradox in managing new product development. *Strategic Management Journal, 13*(S1), 111–125.

Machlup, F. (1983). *The study of information: Interdisciplinary messages.* http://philpapers.org/rec/MACTSO-9. Accessed 20 February 2015.

Maglitta, J. (1996). Smarten up! *Computerworld, 29*(23), 84–86.

Maina, C. K. (2012). Traditional knowledge management and preservation: Intersections with library and information science. *The International Information & Library Review, 44*(1), 13–27.

Malhotra, Y. (2001). From information management to knowledge management. Beyond the 'hi-tech hidebound' systems. *Knowledge Management and Business Model Innovation.* Idea Group Publishing, 115–134.

Malhotra, Y. (2005). Integrating knowledge management technologies in organizational business processes: getting real time enterprises to deliver real business performance. *Journal of Knowledge Management, 9*(1), 7–28.

Martinez, M. (2004). *Organizzazione, Informazioni e Tecnologie.* Il Mulino: Bologna.

Martinez, M. (2011). ICT, productivity and organizational complementarily. In A. Carugati & C. Rossignoli (Eds.), *Emerging themes in information systems and organization studies* (pp. 271–280). Heidelberg: Physica-Verlag.

Marwick, A. (2001). *The new nature of history: Knowledge, evidence, language.* Chicago: Lyceum Books, Incorporated.

McQueen, R. (1998). Four views of knowledge and knowledge management. In *AMCIS 1998 Proceedings,* 204.

Nelson, R. R., & Winter, S. G. (1982). *An evolutionary theory of economic change.* Cambridge: Belknap Press.

Nonaka, I. (1991). The knowledge-creating company. *Harvard Business Review, 69,* 96–104.

Nonaka, I. (1994). A dynamic theory of organizational knowledge creation. *Organization Science, 5*(1), 14–37.

Nonaka, I., & Konno, N. (1998). The concept of 'Ba': Building a foundation for knowledge creation. *California Management Review, 40,* 40–55.

Nonaka, I., & Takeuchi, H. (1995). *The knowledge- creating company: How Japanese companies create the dynamics of innovation.* New York: Oxford University Press.

Nonaka, I., & Toyama, R. (2002). A firm as a dialectical being: Towards a dynamic theory of a firm. *Industrial and Corporate Change, 11*(5), 995–1009.

Nonaka, I., & Toyama, R. (2003). The knowledge-creating theory revisited: Knowledge creation as a synthesizing process. *Knowledge Management Research & Practice, 1*(1), 2–10.

Nonaka, I., Toyama, R., & Konno, N. (2000). SECI, Ba and leadership: A unified model of dynamic knowledge creation. *Long Range Planning, 33*(1), 5–34.

Nonaka, I., & Von Krogh, G. (2009). Perspective-tacit knowledge and knowledge conversion: Controversy and advancement in organizational knowledge creation theory. *Organization Science, 20*(3), 635–652.

Nonaka, I., von Krogh, G., & Voepel, S. (2006). Organizational knowledge creation theory: Evolutionary paths and future advances. *Organization Studies, 27*(8), 1179–1208.

O'Dell, C., & Grayson, C. J. (1998). If only we knew what we know: Identification and transfer of internal best practices. *California Management Review, 40*(3), 154–174.

Orlikowski, W. J. (2002). Knowing in practice: Enacting a collective capability in distributed organizing. *Organization Science, 13*(3), 249–273.

Panahi, S., Watson, J., & Partridge, H. (2013). Towards tacit knowledge sharing over social web tools. *Journal of Knowledge Management, 17*(3), 379–397.

Penrose, E. T. (1959). *The theory of the growth of the firm.* New York: Wiley.

Pezzillo Iacono, M., Martinez, M., Mangia, G., & Galdiero, C. (2012). Knowledge creation and inter-organizational relationships: The development of innovation in the railway industry. *Journal of Knowledge Management, 16*(4), 604–616.

Polanyi, M. (1958). *Personal knowledge.* Chicago: University of Chicago Press.

Polanyi, M. (1962). *Personal knowledge: Toward a post-critical philosophy.* New York: Harper Torchbooks.

Polanyi, M. (1966). *The tacit dimension.* New York: Doubleday.

Polanyi, M. (1967). *The tacit dimension.* London: Routledge and Keoan Paul.

Prahalad, C. K., & Hamel, G. (1994). Strategy as a field of study: Why search for a new paradigm? *Strategic Management Journal, 15*(S2), 5–16.

Probst, G. (1998). Practical knowledge management: A model that works. *PRISM-CAMBRIDGE MASSACHUSETTS-,* 17–30.

Probst, G., Raub, S., & Romhardt, K. (2006). *Bausteine des Wissensmanagements.* Wiesbaden: Gabler.

Probst, G., & Romhardt, K. (1997). Building blocks of knowledge management—A practical approach. Input-Paper for the seminar: *"Knowledge Management and the European Union-Towards a European Knowledge Union",* 12–14 May 1997 at Utrecht, Kennis Centrum/Dutch Ministry for Education.

Romhardt, K. (1997). Processes of knowledge preservation: Away from a technology dominated approach. In *Proceedings der 21, "Deutschen Jahrestagung für Künstliche Intelligenz",* 9.

Sandelands, L. E., & Stablein, R. E. (1987). The concept of organization mind. *Research in the Sociology of Organizations, 5,* 135–161.

Schiavone, F., & Agrifoglio, R. (2012). Communities of practice and practice preservation: A case study. In M. De Marco, D. Te'eni, V. Albano, & S. Za (Eds.), *Information systems: Crossroads for organization, management, accounting and engineering.* Berlin: Springer.

Schubert, P., Lincke, D., Schmid, B. (1998). A global knowledge medium as a virtual com-munity: The netacademy concept. In E. Hoadley & I. Benbasat (Eds.), *Proceedings of the Fourth Americas Conference on Information Systems* (pp. 618–620), Baltimore.

Schwartz, D. G., Divitini, M., Brasethvik, T. (2000). On knowledge management in the internet age. In *Internet-based organizational memory and knowledge management,* 1–19.

Sher, P. J., & Lee, V. C. (2004). Information technology as a facilitator for enhancing dynamic capabilities through knowledge management. *Information & Management, 41*(8), 933–945.

Simon, H. A. (1991). Bounded rationality and organizational learning. *Organization Science, 2,* 125–134.

Skok, W., & Kalmanovitch, C. (2005). Evaluating the role and effectiveness of an intranet in facilitating knowledge management: A case study at Surrey county council. *Information & Management, 42*(5), 731–744.

Spender, J. C. (1994). Organizational knowledge, collective practice and penrose rents. *International Business Review, 3*(4), 353–367.

Spender, J. C. (1996a). Organizational knowledge, learning, and memory: Three concepts in search of a theory. *Journal of Organizational Change Management, 9,* 63–78.

Spender, J. C. (1996b). Making knowledge the basis of a dynamic theory of the firm. *Strategic Management Journal, 17*(S2), 45–62.

Stewart, T. A. (1997). *Intellectual capital.* New York: Currency/Doubleday.

Suchman, L. A. (1987). *Plans and situated actions: The problems of human-machine communication.* Cambridge: Cambridge University Press.

Terret, A. (1998). Knowledge management and the law firm. *Journal of knowledge Management, 2*(1), 67–76.

Tsoukas, H., & Vladimirou, E. (2001). What is organizational knowledge? *Journal of Management Studies, 38*(7), 973–993.

Tuomi, I. (1999). Data is more than knowledge: Implications of the reversed knowledge hierarchy for knowledge management and organizational memory. *Journal of Management Information Systems, 16*(3), 103–117.

Vance, D. M. (1997). Information, knowledge and wisdom: The epistemic hierarchy and computer-based information system. In B. Perkins & I. Vessey (Eds.), *Proceedings of the Third Americas Conference on Information Systems*, Indianapolis.

Von Krogh, G. (1999). *Developing a knowledge-based theory of the firm*. St. Gallen: University of St. Gallen.

Walsh, J. P., & Ungson, G. R. (1991). Organizational memory. *Academy of Management Review, 16*(1), 57–91.

Wasko, M. M., & Faraj, S. (2005). Why should i share? Examining social capital and knowledge contribution in electronic networks of practice. *MIS Quarterly, 29*(S1), 35–57.

Watson, R. T. (1999). *Data management: databases and organizations* (2nd ed.). New York: John Wiley.

Weber, C. K. (1980). *Cognitive and affective influences on text comprehension*. Doctoral dissertation, ProQuest Information & Learning.

Weick, K. E. (1991). The nontraditional quality of organizational learning. *Organization Science, 2*, 116–123.

Weick, K. E., & Roberts, K. H. (1993). Collective mind and organizational reliability: The case of flight operations on an aircraft carrier deck. *Administrative Science Quarterly, 38*, 357–381.

Wigg, K. M. (1997). Integrating intellectual capital and knowledge management. *Long Range Planning, 30*(3), 399–405.

Wijnhoven, F. (2003). Operational Knowledge management: Identification of knowledge objects, operation methods, and goals and means for the support function. *Journal of the Operational Research Society, 54*(2), 194–203.

Zack, M. H. (1999). Managing codified knowledge. *Sloan Management Review, 40*(4), 45–58.

Chapter 2
Communities of Practice

Abstract This chapter reviews the literature on community of practice. Although the relevance of this form of aggregation in information systems (IS) research and organizational literature is just emerging, communities of practice have always and still do exist everywhere in every aspect of human and work life, both inside and outside organizational boundaries. After defining the concept of community of practice and reviewing its different forms, this chapter looks inside the community in order to understand certain clearly identified characteristics, such as the domain, the community and the practice. Finally, it also explores knowledge management in communities of practice by highlighting the processes of creating and sharing knowledge, and by introducing those of knowledge preservation.

Keywords Community of practice · Types of community of practice · Knowledge management processes · Knowledge creation and sharing · Knowledge preservation

2.1 Defining Community of Practice

What is a community of practice? Defining community of practice (CoP) is not an easy task. Many academics and practitioners have addressed this issue, defining the concept in different ways. Although the term has been coined in recent years, the phenomenon is not new but refers to an age-old idea. According to Jean Lave, a cognitive anthropologist, and Etienne Wenger, an educational theorist and computer scientist, CoPs have existed for as long as people have been learning and sharing their experiences through storytelling. Some examples are the first knowledge-based social structures, back when humans lived in caves; the corporations in ancient Rome; artisans in the Middle Ages; physicians and nurses, or priests and nuns, in the late Middle Ages and afterwards; communities related to organizations and industries, whether formally recognized or not, in more recent times; etc. More generally, as Lave and Wenger (1991) assumed, communities of

© The Author(s) 2015
R. Agrifoglio, *Knowledge Preservation Through Community of Practice*,
SpringerBriefs in Information Systems, DOI 10.1007/978-3-319-22234-9_2

practice have always and still do exist everywhere in every aspect of human life.[1] "We all belong to a number of them—at work, at school, at home, in our hobbies. Some have a name, some don't. Some we recognize, some remain largely invisible. We are core members of some and occasional participants in others. Whatever form our participation takes, most of us are familiar with the experience of belonging to a community of practice" (Wenger et al. 2002, p. 5).

Lave and Wenger (1991) have defined the CoP as a group of people who come together to share common interests and goals, with the aim of sharing information, developing knowledge and developing themselves both personally and professionally. Other definitions of community of practice are: "groups of people who share a concern, a set of problems, or a passion about a topic, and who deepen their knowledge and expertise in this area by interacting on an ongoing basis" (Wenger et al. 2002, p. 4), and "a group of people informally bound together by shared expertise and passion for a joint enterprise" (Wenger and Snyder 2000, p. 139). People join communities for several reasons, such as education, professional issues, and hobbies. Within such a community, people share their experience and tacit knowledge in free flow, improving their abilities and skills, and fostering learning. CoP members explore ideas, discuss situations and needs, and help each other solve problems, although they do not meet every day. Each person has their own experience; CoP simply allows them to share such experience with other members when they meet. Unlike teams and organizational units, CoPs are self-organizing systems whose methods of interaction, rules, issues and lifespan are determined by members, based on the intrinsic value that membership brings (Sharratt and Usoro 2003; Metallo 2007). Such communities are not constrained by time and space and therefore emerge as effective loci for engaging directly in activities, conversations, and other forms of personal participation in social life (Lave and Wenger 1991; Wenger 1998; Wenger et al. 2002). Community members develop common sets of codes and language, share norms and values, carry out critical reflection, and engage in dialog with each other at a professional level, generating an environment characterized by high levels of trust, shared behavioral norms, and mutual respect and reciprocity (Sharratt and Usoro 2003). This environment has been directly linked to knowledge creation and sharing processes. Katzy and Ma (2002) argue that both the community and community members (e.g., developers, teachers, lawyers, doctors, academics and consultants) themselves could add value to the status quo in terms of knowledge creation, knowledge sharing, and identification. Indeed, people join a community to develop knowledge and specific expertise about a particular issue, which could not be obtained otherwise (e.g., Wenger and Snyder 2000; Wenger et al. 2002; Metallo 2007).

Although Lave and Wenger (1990, 1991) are recognized as the pioneers of CoP research, the phenomenon was simultaneously investigated by Brown and

---

[1] For more details see the seminal work of Durkheim (1893), *De La Division Du Travail Social: étude sur l'organisation des sociétés supérieures* (well-known as The Division of Labor in Society), who traced the history of professional groups (often communities) over time.

Duguid (1991), and even earlier by Orr (1990), by Constant (1987) and by Lave (1988) herself. Indeed, the term "community of practice" was first mentioned by Lave and Wenger (1991) in their book on situated learning, but the idea has existed since Homo sapiens evolved 50,000 years ago and the phenomenon has been investigated with reference to research on the relationship between knowledge and work practice. As we will see later, practice plays a crucial role in defining CoP and developing a view of learning as social construction. In order to trace and understand the evolution of the concept of CoP, we need to focus particularly on three major publications: Lave and Wenger (1991), Wenger (1998), and Wenger et al. (2002).

According to Lave and Wenger (1991), a CoP is defined as a group of people who come together to share common interests and goals aimed at improving their skills by working alongside more experienced members and being involved in increasingly complicated tasks. The community is a locus that enables a newcomer to learn by engaging in simple tasks, assisted by comparatively or highly experienced people (the latter being commonly known as old-timers). Initially, newcomers become acquainted with the tasks, norms, values and principles of the community and then gradually increase their participation and involvement in community life. Authors have referred to the journey from being a newcomer to becoming an expert as "legitimate peripheral learning" and the underlying model of learning as "situated learning." Unlike the old model of learning based on a mechanistic process of cognitive transmission, the new model as proposed by Lave and Wenger (1990, 1991) tends toward the logic of constructivism, which relies on social interaction at the workplace. According to this model, learning occurs in social relationships with other learners by observation and peripheral participation in the community rather than in a classroom setting. Indeed, "Legitimate peripheral participation provides a way to speak about the relations between newcomers and old-timers, and about activities, identities, artefacts, and communities of knowledge and practice. A person's intentions to learn are engaged and the meaning of learning is configured through the process of becoming a full participant in a sociocultural practice. This social process includes, indeed it subsumes, the learning of knowledgeable skills" (Lave and Wenger 1991, p. 29). Learning is, thus, "an evolving, continuously renewed set of relations" (Lave and Wenger 1991, p. 50) or, more simply, a process of social participation where the nature of the situation impacts significantly on the process itself. However, although situated learning has been a very influential corrective to previous educational methods, the contribution of individual learning continues to be recognized, as well as the validity of educational paradigm (Cox 2005).

Then, Wenger (1998) focuses on the role of the social interactive dimension of situated learning and expands the concept of CoP. According to the author, CoP refers to three dimensions: joint enterprise (*what it is about*), mutual engagement (*how it functions*), and shared repertoire (*what capability it has produced*). Joint enterprise is a joint purpose for joint action, or perhaps the higher levels of action in the job. The term joint enterprise does not merely refer to shared goals, but a negotiated enterprise, and involves mutual accountability (Wenger 1998). More specifically, joint enterprise is defined as the process in which people are engaged and working together toward a common goal (Li et al. 2009). Mutual engagement, on the other hand, refers to norms and social interactions built by community members and leads to the creation of shared meaning on issues or problems. According to Wenger (1998), relationships of mutual engagement bind the members of the community together into a social entity. Mutual engagement plays a crucial role in CoP, representing building blocks in the functioning of the community itself. Finally, shared repertoire concerns the common resources (routines, sensibilities, artifacts, stories, vocabulary, styles, etc.) that members use to negotiate meaning and facilitate learning within the community. In this regard, a CoP is defined as a group of people who communicate with each other (mutual engagement) and develop ways and resources (shared repertoire) for reaching a common goal (joint enterprise). Based on these three dimensions (known also as community domains), Wenger (1998) also proposes 14 indicators for detecting the presence of CoP.[2] Table 2.1 shows the 14 indicators identifying community of practice.

Among these indicators, only two concern joint enterprise and most are abstract. However, although Wenger's (1998) book has raised controversies about the definition of CoP, it also helps identify the central role of "practice" within community. "Any community of practice produces abstractions, tools, symbols, stories, terms, and concepts that reify something of that practice in a congealed form" (Wenger 1998, p. 59). This process, known as reification, allows us to give form to experience by perceiving it as an object. Within communities, "meaning is negotiated through a process of participation and reification" (Wenger 1998, p. 55).

Another important contribution to the CoP debate has been provided by Wenger et al. (2002), authors of the book *Cultivated Communities of Practice*. As Cox (2005) suggests, with this book Wenger marks a decisive shift in his own writing into a different discourse, moving the focus from a social perspective, in term of individuals' learning and identity development, to a managerialist conception of community. CoP is vaguely defined as "groups of people who share a concern, a set of problems, or a passion about a topic, and who deepen their knowledge and expertise in this area by interacting on an ongoing basis" (Wenger et al. 2002, p. 4). Although this definition is vaguer than the previous 14 indicators used to identify CoP, it does not limit communities to groups within a company. Instead, community becomes a tool for organizations, which can engineer and cultivate CoPs aiming to enhance workers' knowledge. Cultivating community means fostering existing ties to create new groupings of people who, ignoring the formal boundaries of organization, work

---

[2]Some critiques of Wenger's conceptualization of CoP have been advanced by Cox (2005), who believes the use of the term community is not appropriate to describe the emergent relationships around a practice. Based on sociological thinking, Cox (2005) states that the term community is not clearly definable and that Wenger's conceptualization is paradoxical in the history of that term. For instance, unlike Wenger, Cox (2005) argues that CoP is not necessarily friendly or harmonious (Indicator 1); a group is based on a practice not a locality (Indicator 7); a group of people who differ, having different skills and knowledge and "mutually defining identities" (Indicator 8). Further arguments are summarized in research by Roberts (2006), whose review of critiques of the CoP approach focuses more on variables of power, trust, and predispositions.

Table 2.1 The 14 indicators identifying community of practice

Wenger's indicators	CoP domains
1. Sustained mutual relationships—harmonious or conflictual	Mutual engagement
2. Shared ways of engaging in doing things together	Mutual engagement Joint enterprise
3. The rapid flow of information and propagation of innovation	Mutual engagement
4. Absence of introductory preambles, as if conversations and interactions were merely the continuation of an ongoing process	Mutual engagement Shared repertoire
5. Very quick setup of a problem to be discussed	Mutual engagement Shared repertoire
6. Substantial overlap in participants' descriptions of who belongs	Mutual engagement
7. Knowing what others know, what they can do, and how they can contribute to an enterprise	Mutual engagement Joint enterprise
8. Mutually defining identities	Mutual engagement
9. The ability to assess the appropriateness of actions and products	Shared repertoire
10. Specific tools, representations, and other artefacts	Shared repertoire
11. Local lore, shared stories, inside jokes, knowing laughter	Shared repertoire
12. Jargon and shortcuts to communication as well as the ease of producing new ones	Shared repertoire Mutual engagement
13. Certain styles recognized as displaying membership	Mutual engagement
14. A shared discourse reflecting a certain perspective on the world	Mutual engagement

Source Wenger (1998, p. 125)

together to share knowledge and creatively solve problems (Cox 2005). Thus, communities of practice provide value through their ability to improve business outcomes (short term) and to develop organizational capabilities (long term), coming out as a way to realize business strategy (Wenger et al. 2002). With respect to previous research, Wenger and colleagues also revise the CoP characteristics into "*domain* of knowledge, which defines a set of issues, *community* of people who care about this domain, and the shared *practice* that they are developing to be effective in their domain" (p. 27). Using these three constituent elements for defining CoP as a social structure, the authors also clarify "*what is not a community of practice*," pointing out the differences from other types such as functional units, operational teams, informal networks, communities of interest, and professional associations. Distinctions between CoP and other structures are reported in Table 2.2.

Although such distinction is useful for teaching purpose, the results are too unclear and contradictory for research (see Li et al. 2009). For example, the difference between CoP and community of interest appear too vague for Fischer (2001), who distinguishes two types of communities: homogeneous (known as CoP), consisting of members from a single discipline; and heterogeneous (known as community of interest or community-of-communities), which refers to a multidisciplinary team. Communities of interest, as Fischer (2001, p. 4) suggests, "bring together stakeholders from different CoPs to solve a particular (design) problem of common concern." In this regard, a community of interest should be regarded as a variation on a CoP rather than something else.

Table 2.2 Communities of practice and other structures

	What's the purpose?	Who belongs?	How clear are the boundaries?	What holds them together?	How long do they last?
Communities of practice	To create, expand, and exchange knowledge, and to develop individual capabilities	Self-selection based on expertise or passion for a topic	Fuzzy	Passion, commitment, and identification with the group and its expertise	Evolve and end organically (last as long as there is relevance to the topic and value and interest in learning together)
Formal departments	To deliver a product or service	Everyone who reports to the group's manager	Clear	Job requirements and common goals	Intended to be permanent (but last until the next reorganization)
Operational teams	To take care of an ongoing operation or process	Membership assigned by management	Clear	Shared responsibility for the operation	Intended to be ongoing (but last as long as the operation is needed)
Project teams	To accomplish a specified task	People who have a direct role in accomplishing the task	Clear	The project's goals and milestones	Predetermined ending (when the project has been completed)
Community of interest	To be informed	Whoever is interested	Fuzzy	Access to information and sense of like-mindedness	Evolve and end organically
Informal networks	To receive and pass on information, to know who is who	Friends and business acquaintances, friends of friends	Undefined	Mutual need and relationships	Never really start or end (exist as long as people keep in touch or remember each other)

Source Wenger et al. (2002, p. 42)

2.2 Types of Community of Practice

Communities of practice can take different forms. Knowing the variations among CoPs is important for better understanding "what it is" and "what it is not," as well as the organizational setting. Although it is an interesting issue, few contributors have tried to investigate the typologies of CoP (e.g., McDermott 2000a, b; APQC 2001; Fischer 2001; Gongla and Rizzuto 2001; Wenger et al. 2002; Dubé et al. 2006;

Metallo 2007). In particular, the research of McDermott (2000a, b) and APQC (2001) focuses on the initial purposes that lead people to join or develop communities or organizations. Fischer's study (2001), by contrast, investigates communities according to the type undertaking similar work (or their cultural background), so distinguishing the CoP (homogeneous community) from the community-of-communities (heterogeneous community).

Gongla and Rizzuto (2001) focus on CoPs within organizational boundaries, and IBM in particular, as well as on their stages of evolution. Such communities are defined as an institutionalized knowledge network; that is, an informal network of professionals managing domains of knowledge within organizations (Gongla and Rizzuto 2001).

A more comprehensive taxonomy of communities of practice is provided by Wenger et al. (2002) and Dubé et al. (2006). In particular, it must be acknowledged that the study of Wenger et al. (2002) seems to be the first to offer a wide classification of the forms of CoP. The authors identify a different typology of communities, such as small/big, short-lived/long-lived, co-located/distributed, homogeneous/heterogeneous, inside boundaries/across boundaries, spontaneous/intentional, and unrecognized/institutionalized (Wenger et al. 2002, pp. 24–27). While the literature recognizes the initial effort to identify and categorize the various forms of community, some criticisms later emerge, related to (1) the comprehensiveness of the taxonomy and (2) the exclusion of technology as a driver for the classification.

Finally, a more recent contribution tries to overcome the limits of Wenger et al. (2002) research, so offering a more comprehensively articulated taxonomy of the forms of CoP (Dubé et al. 2006). In contrast to Wenger et al. (2002) research, the study of Dubé et al. (2006) focuses more on a specific type of CoP, i.e. virtual CoP, pointing out the crucial role of technology in today's communities.

Based on these researches, I have looked again at the forms identifying the categories and features that lead to their composition as well as the main contributions related to the theme. Table 2.3 shows the variety of forms of CoP.

Thus, to identify the various forms of CoP, we select the nine most meaningful structural features and classify them into four categories: demographic, organizational, individual and technological.

With reference to the "demographic category," I identify the following three types of community:

1. *Young or old*: age defines the period of time the CoP has been in existence. In this regard, we can place the duration of the CoP along a continuum from young (less than a year) to old (more than five years). Some scholars (Gongla and Rizzuto 2001; Dubé et al. 2006) find a relationship between the age of a community and its level of maturity (commonly known as stage of community development). Based on previous research, Dubé et al. (2006) distinguish five stages of development: potential, coalescing, maturing, stewardship and trans-formation; and assume that young communities are usually in the early stages, while old communities are in later ones.

Table 2.3 Forms of community of practice

Categories	Features	Forms of community of practice	Support from literature
Demographic	Age	Young/old	Gongla and Rizzuto (2001), Dubé et al. (2006)
	Size	Small/big	Von Krogh (2002), Wenger et al. (2002), Dubé et al. (2006)
	Lifespan	Short-lived/long-lived	Wenger et al. (2002), Dubé et al. (2006)
Organizational	Creation process	Spontaneous/intentional	McDermott (2000a, b), APQC (2001), Wenger et al. (2002), Dubé et al. (2006)
	Organizational boundaries	Inside boundaries/across boundaries	APQC (2001), Gongla and Rizzuto (2001), Wenger et al. (2002)
	Degree of formalization	Unrecognized/institutionalized	APQC (2001), Gongla and Rizzuto (2001), Wenger et al. (2002)
Individual	Proximity	Co-located/distributed	Wenger et al. (2002), Dubé et al. (2006), Metallo (2007)
	Background	Homogeneous/heterogeneous	Fischer (2001), Wenger et al. (2002)
Technological	Degree of reliance on ICT	Face-to-face/virtual	Dubé et al. (2006), Metallo (2007)

2. *Small or big*: CoPs are "small" or "big" depending on the number of members involved in them. Although their size can change, it is not yet clearly distinguished in the literature. Wenger et al. (2002), indeed, assume that small communities involve only a few specialists, while big communities consist of hundreds of people. Other research links size with organizational issues in terms of active community participation, individual interest, social relationships, and contribution (e.g., Von Krogh 2002; Dubé et al. 2006). Although both communities usually comprise a core group of members who contribute actively, plus peripheral members, the size does matter. For instance, "a large community is more likely to include people with contingent, diverse, and distributed interests, and social relationships may become ephemeral" (Dubé et al. 2006, p. 78).

3. *Short-lived or long-lived*: the lifespan of a CoP varies from short-lived (temporary) to long-lived (permanent). Some communities of practice, such as artisans, boat makers, etc., exist over centuries because they are created on a permanent basis with no definite time frame in mind (Wenger et al. 2002; Dubé et al. 2006). Others, such as COBOL programmers, are assembled on a temporary basis to accomplish a specific purpose (Wenger et al. 2002;

Dubé et al. 2006). Thus, the first type can be defined as "long-lived," while the latter are "short-lived" communities.

With reference to "organizational category," the following three types of community are identified:

1. *Spontaneous or intentional*: Communities of practice have existed for ages, born in response to people's spontaneous need to group, share ideas, and be helped (McDermott 1999; Wenger et al. 2002; Dubé et al. 2006). Communities of artisans, boat makers, violin makers, gangs of street cleaners, etc. are common examples of spontaneous communities. On the other hand, communities are also launched to meet the needs of organizations for specific knowledge and skill resources. These types may be intentionally established by management, who also define the community's purpose and select key members (Dubé et al. 2006). At other times, however, communities emerge spontaneously on the initiative of their members and are then recognized and accepted by management.

2. *Inside boundaries or across boundaries*: Communities of practice often exist either entirely within organizations (inside boundaries), and in particular within a business unit or across business units, or across organizational boundaries (across boundaries) (Wenger et al. 2002). Organizations can decide to promote collaboration, social relationships and knowledge sharing by establishing CoPs that cross boundaries across work groups, organizational units and even organizations (Wenger and Snyder 2000; Dubé et al. 2006). Across-boundaries communities allow a greater number of people to join. However, a low level of boundary crossing may also facilitate interaction among community members, as well as the exchange of ideas and knowledge sharing.

3. *Unrecognized or institutionalized*: Workers may join communities that are completely formalized, less formalized or not formalized within organizations. According to Wenger et al. (2002, p. 27), with reference to the degree of institutionalized formalism, CoPs vary in their relationships to organizations, ranging from unrecognized (invisible to the organization), bootlegged (visible only to certain groups), legitimized (taken into account by the organization), supported (receiving direct resources) to institutionalized (given an official status and function in the organization). When a CoP is institutionalized within the organization, it could be considered a formal unit like other business units or divisions.

With reference to individual categories, the features related to proximity of relationships and cultural background lead us to identify two additional forms of communities: co-located/distributed and homogeneous/heterogeneous.

1. *Co-located versus distributed*: The proximity of relationships or geographic dispersion among members is a useful characteristic for distinguishing co-located as opposed to distributed CoPs. Communities are co-located when members usually meet at the same place or live nearby. Although working together requires regular interaction, co-location is not a necessity (Wenger et al.

2002). Indeed, an increasing amount of evidence shows communities whose members are not physically located in the same place, but scattered around the world. Communities of scientists, for instance, whose members work for different organizations around the world, regular meet to discuss specific research topics thanks to seminars, conferences and ad hoc meetings held at the same building. However, when communities are distributed, face-to-face meetings, and thus chances to exchange ideas and share knowledge, become more complicated and expensive for members. ICT and remote-working technologies, as we will see later, provide a valid solution for such communities.

2. *Homogeneous or heterogeneous*: Communities can be distinguished on the basis of members' cultural background (Wenger et al. 2002). Indeed, communities are often composed of people from the same discipline or function (homogeneous). Sometimes, instead, communities are composed of members with different backgrounds (heterogeneous). Other research (Dubé et al. 2006) also links cultural influence with the background of community members. According to Dubé et al. (2006), cultural influence in national, organizational and professional terms is evaluated along a continuum from homogeneous to heterogeneous. Communities are homogeneous where members have similar backgrounds because they come from the same organization, or different organizations with similar cultures, and live in a country with a strongly localized culture. On the other hand, communities are heterogeneous where members have different backgrounds because they come from various organizations and live in a country with a more open culture or with different cultures.

The last category is technological. Within this category, it is possible to distinguish face-to-face and virtual (often known as web-based) communities based on the degree of reliance on ICT. These two types of community are described below.

1. *Face-to-face community versus virtual community*: new technologies, and above all those developed for supporting remote workers, have created new ways to interact and communicate for community members who used to meet exclusively face-to-face. Older communities in which members usually carried out their practice in the same organization or city, or at least in places nearby, have begun to open up to other people around the world thanks to those technologies. ICTs have reduced the spatial (physical space) and temporal (time) distances, enabling people from anywhere and at any time to join the community and perform their practice. More recently, communities have started up on a digital basis and allow members to join, interact and communicate exclusively by using the internet and ICT. Empirical evidence shows that some communities work without ICT support (known as face-to-face communities); some exclusively use ICT (well-known as virtual or online communities); and others use these technologies, but not exclusively. How can we define such hybrid communities? Are they face-to-face or virtual communities? The literature agrees that when a community uses ICT predominantly it can be called "virtual," but otherwise "face-to-face" (e.g., Wenger et al. 2002; Dubé et al. 2006; Metallo 2007).

2.3 Looking Inside Community of Practice

Having defined the concept of CoP and reviewed its different forms, it is right to look inside the community in order to understand certain clearly identified characteristics such as the domain, the community and the practice (Wenger et al. 2002). These three fundamental elements are useful to distinguish communities of practice (as previously defined) from communities (in the broadest sense). As Wenger (2011) states, not all communities are communities of practice. Indeed, a community, in the sense of a group of people who share a concern or passion for something, is a necessary but element for constituting a CoP, but not the only one. Besides the community of people, the domain of knowledge and shared practice are crucial too. Based on the work of Wenger et al. (2002), these three elements are discussed next.

2.3.1 Domain

What is the domain of a CoP? In 1998, Wenger relied on three characteristics, i.e. mutual engagement, shared repertoire and joint enterprise, together known as the community domain, to identify a CoP. In this regard, he defines a CoP as a group of people who communicate with each other (mutual engagement) and develop ways and resources (shared repertoire) for reaching a common goal (joint enterprise). Later, Wenger et al. (2002) revised these three characteristics and named them "domain," "community" and "practice."

According to Wenger et al. (2002), a domain is the area of knowledge that brings the community together and defines a set of issues that members need to address. Within communities, the domain guides the questions, so stimulating members to present their ideas for introducing or contributing to a discussion. It also facilitates the learning process among people. In this regard, the domain creates "the common ground (i.e., the minimal competence that differentiates members from non-members) and outlines the boundaries that enable members to decide what is worth sharing and how to present their ideas" (Li et al. 2009, p. 6).

As well as defining common ground, the domain also defines a sense of common identity. As situated learning theory suggests, learning also concerns a process of understanding who we are and in which CoP we belong. When acting in a community, people develop a sense of membership and are more inclined to identify with the community itself. Within CoPs, like other groups, people feel they belong to a community and are accepted by others with whom they share the practice, so developing a sense of commitment to structure and identity in their relationships (Handley et al. 2006). As Wenger (2004) suggested, within CoPs, identity is not defined by a task, as it would be within a team, but by an area of knowledge that needs to be explored and developed.

2.3.2 Community

While the domain creates the common ground of a CoP, the community refers to the social structures that encourage learning through interaction and relationships among members. As Wenger et al. (2002) suggest, community is a crucial element for an effective knowledge structure. Besides knowledge sharing and practice, a community is composed of people who interact and build interpersonal relationships on issues important to their domain.

Interpersonal relationships are the foundation upon which the community evolves. A community is a place in which people help each other augment their knowledge about a specific practice. Social relationships, especially if kept up regularly, enable discussion and debate among community members on issues within a domain, fostering ideas and developing a sense of belonging and commitment. The social dimension, thus, is a necessary but not sufficient condition to build a CoP. To build a CoP, as Wenger et al. (2002) assume, the interactions among members must have some continuity. For example, people who meet sporadically to discuss a particular topic do not constitute a CoP. To build a community the interactions must be regular, so enabling members to develop a shared understanding of their domain and an approach to their practice (Wenger 1998; Wenger et al. 2002).

The role of social relationships within CoPs has also been explored by other research (Lesser and Prusak 1999). Based on social capital theory, Lesser and Prusak (1999, p. 2) assume that "Communities of Practice are valuable to organizations because they contribute to the development of social capital, which in turn is a necessary condition for knowledge creation, sharing and use." According to Nahapiet and Ghoshal (1998), social capital is the sum of the actual and potential resources embedded within, available through, and derived from the network of relationships possessed by an individual or social unit.

2.3.3 Practice

Finally, another crucial element for constituting a CoP is the practice itself. According to Wenger et al. (2002), the practice is a set of shared repertoires of resources that include experiences, stories, tools, and ways of addressing recurring problems. Rather than a community of interest, members of a CoP are practitioners, and thus develop a shared repertoire of resources. For this reason, the practice is nothing more than the specific knowledge owned, developed and shared by members within a CoP.

Based on the concept of practice developed by Wenger, some academic scholars show that this concept draws on different intellectual backgrounds and, thus, is wider and more ambiguous than Wenger assumes (e.g., Knorr Cetina 1999). In effect, the concept of practice is stressed by some scholars who try to trace the similarities and differences in definitions and meanings (e.g., Cook and Brown 1999; Gherardi 2000; Nicolini et al. 2003; Corradi et al. 2010). Among them, the research of Corradi et al. (2010) reviews the academic research on the concept of practice in studies of organizing, learning and knowing over the last 20 years, in order to identify the different labels and meanings. In particular, Corradi and colleagues distinguish the concept of practice in two ways: as an "empirical object" and as "a way of seeing," and identify conceptual labels for each of them.

Practice as an empirical object refers to "the locus in which scholars study the activities of the practitioners" (Corradi et al. 2010, p. 268). This concept of practice includes three principal interpretative labels: "practice-based standpoint" (Brown and Duguid 1991), "work-based learning" or "practice-based learning" (e.g., Raelin 1997; Strati 2007), and practice as "what people do" (e.g., Whittington 1996). Following Marx work, Orr (1990) and Lave and Wenger (1990), Brown and Duguid (1991) stress the concept of practice by showing the link between practice and learning within a "situated" organizational context, such as a CoP. In this regard, practice refers to "learning-in-working," which "best represents the fluid evolution of learning through practice" (Brown and Duguid 1991, p. 41). Other scholars, instead, have investigated the link between practice and social and collective learning arising from observation, discussion and action in different organizational contexts (e.g., Raelin 1997, 2007) and, in particular in both face-to-face and virtual communities of practice (e.g., Strati 2007; Nicolini 2007; Alvino et al. 2011). Finally, some research focuses on science as practice (e.g., Pickering 1990) and on strategy as practice (e.g., Whittington 1996), emphasizing what scientists and managers do.

Practice as "a way of seeing" a context moves toward "a more explicit acknowledgement of practice as epistemology" (Corradi et al. 2010, p. 273). In respect of practice as an "empirical object," Corradi et al. (2010) identify four other labels with reference to practice as "a way of seeing." These are "practice lens or practice-oriented research" (e.g., Orlikowski 2000; Østerlund and Carlile 2005), "knowing-in-practice" (e.g., Gherardi 2000; Orlikowski 2002), "practice-based perspective" (e.g., Sole and Edmondson 2002), and "practice-based approach" (e.g., Carlile 2002). The first label refers to Orlikowski's research (2002) aimed at rethinking the concept of technology in organizations. Based on the Giddens' Structuration Theory (1979, 1984), Orlikowski (2002) develops a new model to examine the interaction between technology and organizations, known as the duality of technology. This model assumes that technology is physically and socially constructed by people working in a social context and by the different meanings they attach to it, so allowing us to see it as a social practice enacted by human action and institutionalized in structure. Similarly, Østerlund and Carlile (2005) focus on practice-oriented research to explain knowledge sharing within a CoP. Practice is not only what people do within a specific context, but is also the locus for production and reproduction of social relations. Within CoPs, indeed, knowledge resides in both practices and social relations. Knowing-in-practice is a concept developed by Gherardi in 2000, based on the idea that knowledge is not something in people's heads, but is constructed by practicing in a context of interaction. Practice in a context is a way to enable people to acquire knowledge (Gherardi 2000; Orlikowski 2000; Nicolini et al. 2003). Practice-based perspective, instead, is a lens able to highlight the "knowledge grounded in site-specific work practice" (Sole and Edmondson 2002). Based on this perspective, practice is defined as "doing and involves awareness and application of both explicit (language, tools, concepts, roles, procedures) and tacit (rules of thumb, embodied capabilities, shared worldviews) elements. Central to the practice perspective is acknowledgement of the social, historical and structural contexts in which actions take place" (Sole and Edmondson 2002, p. 18). In this regard, practice-based perspective provides additional insights on forms (tacit and explicit) and dimensions (individual and collective) of knowledge developed into a context in which practice is performed (Sole and Edmondson 2002; Swan et al. 2002). Finally, the practice-based approach focuses on how people construct their competence in practice (Carlile 1997, 2002). According to this approach, knowledge is structured in practice and in "objects" (artifacts that individuals work with) and "ends" (outcomes that demonstrate success in creating, measuring, or manipulating objects) that are of consequence in a given practice (Carlile 2002, p. 446).

2.4 Managing Knowledge in Community of Practice

Knowledge is a strategic asset widely recognized by managerial literature, and organizational literature in particular, as a valuable resource for organizational growth and sustained competitive advantage (Miller and Shamsie 1996). In the modern world, faced with competition and increasingly dynamic environments, knowledge has become a crucial resource and a key for survival and success, not only for organizations. As is well known, an organization often does not possess all the knowledge it requires within its boundaries and, thus, it needs to look outside to gain the knowledge it lacks (Anand et al. 2002; Wasko and Faraj 2005; Pezzillo Iacono et al. 2012). For this reason, members of organizations often look for new ways to acquire knowledge from outside. One good way to do this is to create links to external knowledge resources, such as CoPs or networks of practice (Brown and Duguid 2000, 2001; Wasko and Faraj 2005).

Communities of practice, as Brown and Duguid (2001) point out, play a key role in helping maintain a company's competitive advantages for different reasons. Firstly, CoPs are significant repositories for the development, sharing, and preservation of knowledge. According to Wenger, learning is a natural and inevitable aspect of life, and a fundamentally social process. If this is true, we can see CoPs as privileged places for developing, maintaining and sharing useful knowledge for organizations. Moreover, community knowledge is more than the sum of knowledge of its members, because the latter provide social affordances for one another

(Cook and Brown 1999; Brown and Duguid 2001). Finally, community members also carry out their activities in other social contexts, such as organizations and other groups, building bridges between the different structures.

Although CoPs seem to be privileged sites for developing, maintaining, and sharing knowledge, the management of that knowledge is somewhat problematic. Indeed, there are various kinds of knowledge that must be managed in different ways. An interesting review of knowledge has been conducted by Brown and Duguid (2001), who identify various types as well as different approaches for managing them.[3] Knowledge can appear as one or another type (conflicting view), such as explicit or tacit, or both (alternating approach), such as both explicit and tacit. Lindkvist (2005), by contrast, identifies two ideal-type notions of knowledge: knowledge collectivity and knowledge community. The first is related to collectivity of practice, which refers, as the author suggests, to temporary organizations and/or project groups operating within firms consisting of people, most of whom have not met before, who work together to solve a specific problem. Such groups operate in distributed contexts, where the knowledge base is highly dispersed and individualized among members rather than decentered. The second refers to CoPs, where knowledge resides in practice and thus is decentered rather than distributed (Lindkvist 2005).

Although knowledge within CoPs has gained increasing popularity in managerial literature, the management side of knowledge has been less discussed (Wenger 2004). More generally, knowledge management is a system that encompasses various forms of knowledge creation, transfer and storage. With reference to CoP literature, some scholars recognize the importance of the management side of knowledge within a community, addressing their research to one or more forms of knowledge and, thus, using an atomistic rather than systemic approach (Davenport and Prusak 1998; Wasko and Faraj 2000; Gourlay 2001; Walsham 2001; Wenger et al. 2002; Wenger 2004; Ardichvili et al. 2003, 2006). A feeble attempt to understand the process of knowledge management within CoPs by using a systemic approach can be traced back to Wenger (2004), who conceptualizes the doughnut model of knowledge management. This model emphasizes the role of the CoP in the creation and sharing of knowledge among members. Knowledge management is considered to be a strategic activity enabled by the combination of three constituent elements of CoP: domain, community and practice. In this regard, knowledge management is recognized as a recursive and strategic process (doughnut) that allows members to exchange experiences and to build expertise for carrying out work. Interacting regularly, community members share their experiences and learn from each other how to practice better within a specific domain. Although this research recognizes the CoP as a structure for shaping and transferring knowledge, it does not distinguish in depth between the various forms of the process.

---

[3]The knowledge can appear "sticky" and "leaky" (Von Hippel 1994; Liebeskind 1996). Other scholars, by contrast, classify knowledge as "know how" and "know that" or "explicit" and "tacit" (see Brown and Duguid 2001 for a review).

Next we will discuss the process of knowledge management within CoPs with particular reference to its various forms, such as creation, sharing, and preservation of knowledge.

2.4.1 Knowledge Creation and Sharing

Knowledge creation (generation) and sharing (exchange) are considered to be crucial resources for a CoP. The success or failure of a CoP, indeed, is strongly influenced by its ability to accumulate resources and to foster future growth (Ardichvili et al. 2003; Fang and Chiu 2010). A CoP consists of a tightly knit group of members who come together to share common interests and goals, with the aim of sharing information, developing knowledge and developing themselves both personally and professionally (Wenger 1998). Unlike organizations that are very formalized in structure, CoPs are fairly informal entities, often existing only in the mind of their members, who discuss and share the knowledge necessary to solve the problems.[4] Indeed, rather than organizations, the different social systems, organizational culture and climate enable communities to exchange knowledge without much effort and, thus, more easily (Ardichvili et al. 2003). It is no coincidence, in fact, that organizations decide to create and/or support CoPs as a strong alternative to building teams (Nirenberg 1995).

Although I have clarified the role of knowledge creation and sharing in the success or failure of a CoP, the reasons that lead people to create and share knowledge still need to be explained. Prior research has shown that members have various reasons to create and exchange knowledge within a community, ranging from boosting their self-esteem to altruistic and conformist considerations (McLure and Faraj 2000). Based on this research, other scholars have tried to clarify why people are willing to contribute and share their knowledge within a CoP (e.g., Ardichvili et al. 2003, 2006; Wenger 2004; Fang and Chiu 2010).

Ardichvili et al. (2003) have conducted research aimed at understanding the reasons for participation or barriers to participation of people in community life. Active participation of members in community life has been recognized as a necessary condition for knowledge creation and sharing. In particular, the research of Ardichvili et al. (2003) is guided by the following question: what are the reasons (or barriers) for community members to contribute to knowledge creation and sharing? The findings of that research have shown that the majority of people view knowledge as a public good, belonging not to community members but to the whole organization. Thus, the willingness of community members to participate in community life, discussing ideas and exchanging knowledge, is motivated by moral

---

[4]Results of more recent empirical research show that within CoPs the roles, rules and tasks of members are well defined, showing the existence of structures and a hierarchy, even if these are not formalized as organizations (Metallo 2007).

obligation and communal interests rather than self-interest. On the contrary, findings also show that the reasons stopping people from contributing to knowledge generation and exchange are related to their different views of knowledge. Indeed, community members who are not willing to share knowledge view knowledge as a private asset and source of competitive advantage. However, as the authors argue (Ardichvili et al. 2003), such people are in the minority, while others are more willing to create and share knowledge for moral reasons.

Other research, instead, links knowledge creation and sharing with cultural influences (Ardichvili et al. 2006). In particular, such research has aimed to investigate cultural factors influencing knowledge sharing strategies within communities of practice. Findings have shown that cultural factors, such as modesty and competitiveness, negatively influence knowledge sharing within communities of practice. Thus, although such authors recognize the need for deep contributions on the topic, cultural influences determine the willingness (or unwillingness) of community members to create and transfer knowledge.

McLure and Faraj (2005) contribute to this topic by investigating why people share knowledge with others in networks of practice. Although a network of practice is slightly different from a CoP, some results may be generalized. In particular, the findings of such research show that individuals contribute knowledge when "they perceive that it enhances their professional reputations, and to some extent because it is enjoyable to help others" (p. 53).

According to Amin and Roberts (2008), on the other hand, the reasons that lead people to share knowledge and practice arise from interaction and relationships of proximity among community members. Proximity encourages people to interact and to communicate with each other, as well as to forge social ties recognized as crucial for knowledge sharing. If this assumption is established, knowledge sharing among members depends on the kind of community to which they belong. In particular, research has shown that the size (small or large) and the degree of technology usage (traditional or virtual) of a community influence new knowledge generation and sharing among its members (Hall and Graham 2004; Amin and Roberts 2008). Usually, smaller traditional communities of practice are more homogeneous and closed groups rather than larger and virtual ones, so enabling easier communication and greater involvement of members, which fosters the exchange of knowledge and practices. Thus, the social dynamics, and social proximity in particular, are quite different, depending on the various kinds of communities, and affect the ability of people to generate new knowledge and share practices.

Finally, other research agrees that knowledge sharing within a CoP depends on knowledge itself (e.g., Wasko and Faraj 2005; Chiu et al. 2006; Fang and Chiu 2010). According to these authors, knowledge sharing is a bidirectional process that involves both community and members. Indeed, the community accumulates resources and fosters future growth thanks to the sharing of knowledge and practices by its members. Knowledge is the key to sustaining the community as well as being the most valuable resource for its members (Fang and Chiu 2010). For these reasons, knowledge sharing is regarded as a motivation for joining communities.

2.4.2 Knowledge Preservation

As already shown, the academic literature identifies knowledge creation and knowledge sharing as the main reasons that lead individuals to join communities of practice. However, people may decide to join a community for different reasons than those previously identified. Among these reasons, the preservation of knowledge is one of the most important.

The reasons for this choice are very old, dating back to the beginning of human life. For instance, since the Hellenistic period people have used knowledge to build new technologies, such as the "Antikythera mechanism" (about 150 BC) and "stream turbines" (1st century AD), to improve both social life and working activity, sometimes forgetting about the technologies previously used. In both cases, the scientific and technological knowledge that produced these constructions was lost a few decades later, and people rediscovered the ability to build similar mechanisms only a few centuries ago (Schiavone and Agrifoglio 2012). Knowledge has been recognized as a crucial resource for technological advance and people have always sought ways to preserve such knowledge acquired. For instance, academic research on heritage shows that stones, papyrus and books are examples of a wide range of ancient and more recent tools used by people to transfer and store knowledge. Other research focuses on the topic of knowledge management, showing how CoPs contribute to preserving knowledge and practice over time, rather than on knowledge creation and sharing (e.g., Lazaric et al. 2003; Amin and Roberts 2008; Schiavone and Agrifoglio 2012; Agrifoglio and Metallo 2015).

Lazaric et al. (2003) focus on the crucial role of knowledge management, and knowledge articulation and codification in particular, within the steel industry. Such research shows that in the steel industry, local knowledge is often anchored in experts belonging to different communities of practice. According to these authors, such communities play a double role, contributing both to sharing knowledge among members at individual and collective levels and to accumulating and preserving knowledge at different organizational levels. Thus, the main challenge concerns the codification of knowledge that "can only be achieved by making the relevant practices explicit within different communities of practice" (Lazaric et al. 2003, p. 1830).

Amin and Roberts (2008), instead, focus on the role of the CoP in determining learning and knowledge generation across a variety of different working environments. Such research identifies various kinds of CoP (defined as knowing in action) based on their different mode of learning and knowing, such as craft/task-based, professional, epistemic/creative, and virtual. Among these, as the authors suggest, "craft/task-based activities are primarily concerned with replicating and preserving existing knowledge rather than engaging in radical innovation" (Amin and Roberts 2008, p. 359). Within craft/task-based communities, knowledge is codified and embedded within individuals and the sociocultural context and, thus, may be transferred through verbal and physical communication such as co-location, communication in face-to-face meetings, and demonstrations.

Other research, instead, explores knowledge preservation within CoPs based on empirical evidence (Schiavone and Agrifoglio 2012; Agrifoglio and Metallo 2015). Both studies aim to understand the reasons that lead people to join a CoP, showing the explicit contribution of practice preservation (Schiavone and Agrifoglio 2012) and knowledge preservation (Agrifoglio and Metallo 2015), rather than knowledge creation and sharing, in understanding phenomena.

Practice preservation has been defined as "the process by which CoP defends its core practices over time from extinction and obsolescent risks due to external factors" (Schiavone and Agrifoglio 2012, p. 333). Technological and scientific knowledge is never acquired once forever; to achieve new interesting knowledge does not mean that this knowledge will be preserved. For instance, the Multi Arcade Machine Emulator (MAME) is an example of a CoP established to preserve gaming history by preventing vintage games from being lost or forgotten when technological change occurs in the video games industry. In this regard, CoP could be considered a crucial tool for preserving knowledge because it allows the retention of knowledge and technical skills about technology that otherwise might be lost over time. On the other hand, the preservation of practice also allows the creation of new knowledge and technical skills concerning the same technology, with important results for both knowledge preservation and knowledge creation.

Finally, based on the research of Schiavone and Agrifoglio (2012), Agrifoglio and Metallo (2015) focus on the process of knowledge preservation within CoPs. In particular, the study provides evidence on different ways and techniques by which tacit and explicit knowledge is preserved within two different CoPs: the Grecià Salentina (a traditional CoP) and the WoodenBoat (an online CoP). Within the first community, tacit knowledge passes from older to newer generations by popular traditions, storytelling, folk dances and ancient working practices. Within the second, members preserve tacit knowledge by using digital tools, such as a video gallery, web TV and blog, which enable both learning and storage without time and spatial limits. Although such research denotes the natural tendency of CoPs to preserve both tacit and explicit knowledge, less emphasis is given to the preservation of systems and tools of knowledge.

The process of preservation of explicit and tacit knowledge within CoPs, with particular reference to its systems and tools, will be discussed next.

References

Agrifoglio, R., & Metallo, C. (2015). Preserving knowledge through community of practice: A multiple case study. In L. Mola, F. Pennarola & S. Za (Eds.), *From information to smart society* (Vol. 5, pp. 103–111). Lecture Notes in Information Systems and Organisation (LNISO). Berlin: Springer.

Alvino, F., Agrifoglio, R., Metallo, C., & Lepore, L. (2011). Learning and knowledge sharing in virtual communities of practice: A case study. In A. D'Atri (Ed.), *Information technology and innovation trends in organizations* (pp. 425–432). Berlin: Springer.

American Productivity & Quality Center [APQC]. (2001). *Building and sustaining communities of practice: Continuing success in knowledge management.* Houston: Author.

Amin, A., & Roberts, J. (2008). Knowing in action: Beyond communities of practice. *Research Policy, 37,* 353–369.

Anand, V., Glick, W. H., & Manz, C. C. (2002). Thriving on the knowledge of outsiders: Tapping organizational social capital. *The Academy of Management Executive, 16*(1), 87–101.

Ardichvili, A., Maurer, M., Li, W., Wentling, T., & Stuedemann, R. (2006). Cultural influences on knowledge sharing through onlines communities of practice. *Journal of Knowledge Management, 10*(1), 94–107.

Ardichvili, A., Page, V., & Wentling, T. (2003). Motivation and barriers to participation in virtual knowledge-sharing communities of practice. *Journal of knowledge management, 7*(1), 64–77.

Brown, J. S., & Duguid, P. (1991). Organizational learning and communities-of-practice: Toward a unified view of working, learning, and innovation. *Organization Science, 2*(1), 40–57.

Brown, J. S., & Duguid, P. (2000). Mysteries of the region: Knowledge dynamics in Silicon Valley. *The silicon valley edge,* 16–45.

Brown, J. S., & Duguid, P. (2001). Knowledge and organization: A social-practice perspective. *Organization Science, 12*(2), 198–213.

Carlile, P. (1997). *Transforming knowledge in product development: Making knowledge manifest through boundary objects.* Unpublished dissertation, University of Michigan, Ann Arbor, MI.

Carlile, P. R. (2002). A pragmatic view of knowledge and boundaries: Boundary objects in new product development. *Organization Science, 13*(4), 442–455.

Chiu, C., Hsu, M., & Wang, E. T. C. (2006). Understanding knowledge sharing in virtual communities: An integration of social capital and social cognitive theories. *Decision Support Systems, 42*(3), 1872–1888.

Constant, E. (1987). The social locus of technological practice: Community system, or organization. In W. E. Bijker, T. P. Hughes, & T. Pinch (Eds.), *The social construction of technological systems: New directions in the sociology and history of technology.* Cambridge, MA: MIT Press.

Cook, S. D. N., & Brown, J. S. (1999). Bridging epistemologies: The generative dance between organizational knowledge and organizational knowing. *Organization Science, 10*(4), 381–400.

Corradi, G., Gherardi, S., & Verzelloni, L. (2010). Through the practice lens: Where is the bandwagon of practice-based studies heading? *Management Learning, 41*(3), 265–283.

Cox, A. (2005). What are communities of practice? A comparative review of four seminal works. *Journal of Information Science, 31*(6), 527–540.

Davenport, T. H., & Prusak, L. (1998). *Working knowledge: How organizations manage what they know.* Watertown, MA: Harvard Business Press.

Dubé, L., Bourhis, A., & Jacob, R. (2006). Towards a typology of virtual communities of practice. *Interdisciplinary Journal of Information, Knowledge, and Management, 1,* 69–93.

Durkheim, E. (1893). *De la division du travail social: étude sur l'organisation des sociétés supérieures.* F. Alcan.

Fang, Y. H., & Chiu, C. M. (2010). In justice we trust: Exploring knowledge-sharing continuance intentions in virtual communities of practice. *Computers in Human Behavior, 26*(2), 235–246.

Fischer, G. (2001). Communities of interest: Learning through the interaction of multiple knowledge systems. In *Proceedings of the 24th Annual Information Systems Research Seminar in Scandinavia* (pp. 1–14), Ulvik, Norway.

Gherardi, S. (2000). Practice-based theorizing on learning and knowing in organizations: An introduction. *Organization, 7*(2), 211–223.

Giddens, A. (1979). *Central problems in social theory: Action, structure, and contradiction in social analysis.* California: University of California Press.

Giddens, A. (1984). *The constitution of society: Outline of the theory of structuration.* California: University of California Press.

Gongla, P., & Rizzuto, C. R. (2001). Evolving communities of practice: IBM global services experience. *IBM Systems Journal, 40*(4), 842–862.

Gourlay, S. (2001). Knowledge management and HRD. *Human Resource Development International, 4,* 27–46.

Hall, H., & Graham, D. (2004). Creation and recreation: Motivating collaboration to generate knowledge capital in online communities. *International Journal of Information Management, 24,* 235–246.

Handley, K., Sturdy, A., Fincham, R., & Clark, T. (2006). Within and beyond communities of practice: Making sense of learning through participation, identity and practice. *Journal of Management Studies, 43*(3), 641–653.

Katzy, B. R., & Ma, X. (2002). Virtual professional communities-definitions and typology. In *Proceedings of the International Conference on Concurrent Enterprising ICE* (pp. 311–318).

Knorr Cetina, K. (1999). *Epistemic cultures: How the sciences make knowledge.* Cambridge, MA: Harvard University Press.

Lave, J. (1988). *Cognition in practice: Mind, mathematics and culture in everyday life.* Cambridge: Cambridge University Press.

Lave, J., & Wenger, E. (1990). *Situated learning: Legitimate peripheral participation.* Palo Alto, CA: Institute for Research on Learning.

Lave, J., & Wenger, E. (1991). *Situated learning: Legitimate peripheral participation.* Cambridge: Cambridge University Press.

Lazaric, N., Mangolte, P. A., & Massué, M. L. (2003). Articulation and codification of collective know-how in the steel industry: Evidence from blast furnace control in France. *Research Policy, 32*(10), 1829–1847.

Lesser, E., & Prusak, L. (1999). Communities of practice, social capital and organizational knowledge. *Information Systems Review, 1*(1), 3–10.

Li, L. C., Grimshaw, J. M., Nielsen, C., Judd, M., Coyte, P. C., & Graham, I. D. (2009). Use of communities of practice in business and health care sectors: A systematic review. *Implementation Science, 4*(27), 1–9.

Liebeskind, J. B. (1996). Knowledge, strategy, and the theory of the firm. *Strategic Management Journal, 17*(2), 93–109.

Lindkvist, L. (2005). Knowledge communities and knowledge collectivities: A typology of knowledge work in groups. *Journal of Management Studies, 42*(6), 1189–1210.

McDermott, R. (1999). Why information technology inspired but cannot deliver knowledge management. *California Management Review, 41*(4), 103–117.

McDermott, R. (2000a). Knowing in community: 10 critical success factors in building communities of practice. *IHRIM Journal,* 1–12.

McDermott, R. (2000b). Community development as a natural step. *Knowledge Management Review, 3*(5), 16–19.

McLure, M., & Faraj, S. (2000). It is what one does: Why people participate and help others in electronic communities of practice. *The Journal of Strategic Information Systems, 9*(2–3), 55–173.

McLure, M., & Faraj, S. (2005). Why should i share? Examining social capital and knowledge contribution in electronic networks of practice. *MIS Quarterly, 29*(1), 35–57.

Metallo, C. (2007). *L'organizzazione del lavoro a distanza.* Torino: Giappichelli Editore.

Miller, D., & Shamsie, J. (1996). The Resource-based view of the firm in two environments: The hollywood film studios from 1936 to 1965. *Academy of Management Journal, 39*(3), 519–543.

Nahapiet, J., & Ghoshal, S. (1998). Social capital, intellectual capital, and the organizational advantage. *The Academy of Management Review, 23*(2), 242–266.

Nicolini, D. (2007). Stretching out and expanding work practice in time and space: The case of telemedicine. *Human Relations, 60*(6), 889–920.

Nicolini, D., Gherardi, S., & Yanow, D. (2003). *Knowing in organizations: A practice-based Approach.* USA: M. E. Sharpe Inc.

Nirenberg, J. (1995). From team building to community building. *Journal of Organizational Excellence, 22,* 27–30.

Orlikowski, W. J. (2000). Using technology and constituting structures: A practice lens for studying technology in organizations. *Organization Science, 11*(4), 404–428.

Orlikowski, W. J. (2002). Knowing in practice: Enacting a collective capability in distributed organizing. *Organization Science, 13*(3), 249–273.

Orr, J. (1990). Sharing knowledge, celebrating identity: War stories and community memory in a service community. In D. S. Middleton & D. Edwards (Eds.), *Collective remembering: Memory in society*. Beverly Hills, CA: Sage.

Østerlund, C., & Carlile, P. (2005). Relations in practice: Sorting through practice theories on knowledge sharing in complex organizations. *The Information Society, 21*(2), 91–107.

Pezzillo Iacono, M., Martinez, M., Mangia, G., & Galdiero, C. (2012). Knowledge creation and inter-organizational relationships: The development of innovation in the railway industry. *Journal of Knowledge Management, 16*(4), 604–616.

Pickering, A. (1990). Knowledge, practice and mere construction. *Social Studies of Science, 20*(4), 682–729.

Raelin, J. A. (1997). A model of work-based learning. *Organization Science, 8*(6), 563–578.

Raelin, J. A. (2007). Toward an epistemology of practice. *Academy of Management Learning & Education Journal, 6*(4), 495–519.

Roberts, J. (2006). Limits to communities of practice. *Journal of management studies, 43*(3), 623–639.

Schiavone, F., & Agrifoglio, R. (2012). Communities of practice and practice preservation: A case study. In M. De Marco, D. Te'eni, V. Albano & S. Za (Eds.), *Information systems: Crossroads for organization, management, accounting and engineering*. Berlin, Heidelberg: Springer.

Sharratt, M., & Usoro, A. (2003). Understanding knowledge-sharing in online communities of practice. *Electronic Journal on Knowledge Management, 1*(2), 187–196.

Sole, D., & Edmondson, A. (2002). Situated knowledge and learning in dispersed teams. *British Journal of Management, 13*(S2), 17–34.

Strati, A. (2007). Sensible knowledge and practice-based learning. *Management Learning, 38*(1), 61–77.

Swan, J., Scarbrough, H., & Robertson, M. (2002). The construction of 'communities of practice' in the management of innovation. *Management Learning, 33*, 477–496.

Von Hippel, E. (1994). Sticky information and the locus of problem solving: Implications for innovation. *Management Science, 40*(4), 429–439.

Von Krogh, G. (2002). The communal resource and information systems. *Journal of Strategic Information Systems, 11*(2), 85–107.

Walsham, G. (2001). Knowledge management: The benefits and limitations of computer systems. *European Management Journal, 19*(6), 599–608.

Wasko, M. M., & Faraj, S. (2000). It is what one does: Why people participate and help others in electronic communities of practice. *The Journal of Strategic Information Systems, 9*(2), 155–173.

Wasko, M. M., & Faraj, S. (2005). Why should i share? Examining social capital and knowledge contribution in electronic networks of practice. *MIS Quarterly, 29*(S1), 35–57.

Wenger, E. (1998). *Communities of practice: Learning, meaning and identify*. Cambridge, UK: Cambridge University Press.

Wenger, E. (2004). Knowledge management as a doughnut: Shaping your knowledge strategy through communities of practice. *Ivey Business Journal*, 1–8.

Wenger, E. (2011). *Communities of Practice: A brief introduction*. Watertown, MA: Harvard Business Press.

Wenger, E., McDermott, R., & Snyder, W. M. (2002). *Cultivating communities of practice* (1st ed.). Watertown, MA: Harvard Business School Press.

Wenger, E., & Snyder, W. M. (2000). Communities of practice: The organizational frontier. *Harvard Business Review, 78*(1), 139–145.

Whittington, R. (1996). Strategy as practice. *Long Range Planning, 29*(5), 731–735.

Chapter 3
Preserving Knowledge Through Community of Practice

Abstract This chapter investigates knowledge preservation within a community of practice. The emerging relevance of knowledge preservation arises from the issue of loss of knowledge in organizations, which occurs because they are often unable to properly preserve knowledge after acquiring or developing it. Communities of practice provide a natural setting in which cultivating practice in a "social context" enables members to store collective knowledge over time and to recall it in the future. In this regard, communities of practice can be viewed as one of the most effective ways to preserve knowledge over time and distance. This chapter first aims to define and conceptualize "community knowledge preservation" by examining IS research, organizational literature and empirical evidence on communities of practice traced over time. Furthermore, it offers a different and deeper perspective to help us understand the phenomenon by exploring the mechanisms and tools enabling a community of practice to select, store and actualize explicit and tacit forms of collective knowledge.

Keywords Community of practice · Knowledge preservation · Explicit and tacit knowledge · Knowing · Knowledge preservation process · Mechanisms and tools

3.1 Knowledge Preservation Community: Defining and Conceptualizing the Phenomenon

The previous chapter ended by considering the management of knowledge within communities of practice (CoPs), with particular reference to the various aspects of such management, such as the creation, sharing, and preservation of knowledge. According to the IS scholars who have conducted research on the concept of the CoP, knowledge management is considered a recursive and strategic process (doughnut), which allows members to exchange experiences and to build up their expertise. Knowledge and the capability to create and utilize knowledge are considered to be crucial resources within organizations and society.

© The Author(s) 2015   47
R. Agrifoglio, *Knowledge Preservation Through Community of Practice*,
SpringerBriefs in Information Systems, DOI 10.1007/978-3-319-22234-9_3

According to managerial literature, and organizational literature in particular, knowledge is a valuable resource for organizational growth and sustained competitive advantage (Miller and Shamsie 1996). In particular, these studies are based on the view of organization as a system that processes information or solves problems. Within an organization, individuals continually process information and apply knowledge to solve the problems, so developing new knowledge that is useful for further decision-making activity (Malhotra 2005). At the same time, members of a CoP interact regularly with each other, so exchanging information and prior experiences in order to learn how to carry out a practice better within a specific domain. This concept is also stressed by Nonaka (1991, 1994), who focuses on knowledge management within organizations. According to Nonaka (1994), an organization is not merely an information-processing machine, but an entity that creates knowledge through such action and interaction. However, as other authors have assumed (e.g., Anand et al. 2002; Wasko and Faraj 2005), an organization often does not possess all the knowledge it requires within its boundaries and, thus, needs to look outside to find the knowledge it lacks. In this regard, community of practice has been recognized by the IS literature as a social structure for shaping and transferring knowledge (Brown and Duguid 2000, 2001; Wasko and Faraj 2005). As Brown and Duguid (2001) show, a CoP is a privileged place where organizations can develop, maintain and share useful knowledge. Although a great deal has been written about knowledge management within CoPs, this chapter focuses on the process of knowledge preservation, rather than knowledge creation and sharing, so joining the small pool of studies that stress this topic (e.g., Lazaric et al. 2003; Amin and Roberts 2008; Schiavone and Agrifoglio 2012; Agrifoglio and Metallo 2015).

Knowledge preservation is essential to our ability to keep individual know-how available. Although the preservation of knowledge sounds like an obvious and automatic process, this is seldom the case. History is full of examples where people build new technologies that are useful to their work, but forget about those already built. Indeed, historians can show us a wide range of ancient and not-so-ancient tools, where the knowledge and expertise needed to build and use them has been lost time and again. These studies show that after knowledge has been acquired or developed, it must be carefully preserved. Similarly, organizations create knowledge by carrying out their work (corporate memory), but preserving this knowledge is not risk free and they may lose track of it for many reasons (Davidavičienė and Raudeliūnienė 2010). So the topic of knowledge management within organizations, and knowledge preservation in particular, has been recognized as one of the most crucial activities within the organization, because it provides individuals and companies with the basis for creating new knowledge and technical skills (e.g., Mazour 2006; Schiavone and Agrifoglio 2012; Agrifoglio and Metallo 2015).

Among the various tools people use to transfer and preserve knowledge, such as stones, papyrus, ancient books, popular traditions, etc., as heritage and history scholars state, CoPs play a crucial role in preserving knowledge because they allow us to store knowledge and technical skills about a technology that otherwise might be lost over time (e.g., Lazaric et al. 2003; Mazour 2006; Schiavone and Agrifoglio

2012; Agrifoglio and Metallo 2015). Certain empirical and ethnographic evidence underlines the role played by CoPs in this process of knowledge management, and knowledge preservation in particular. For instance, Agrifoglio and Metallo (2015) stress the process of knowledge preservation by describing "the Grecìa Salentina," a small ethnic and linguistic Greek community. Here people speak Griko, sometimes spelled Grico, a form of the Greek language considered to be a modern Greek dialect, which survives today in the Italian region of Apulia. Within this community, people perform songs and poems in the Griko language, allowing current generations to listen to them. They also pass on the ancient working practices needed for their customs and crafts from older to newer generations by allowing the observation of working practice and by storytelling. The case of the Grecìa Salentina community clearly highlights the process of preserving knowledge through interaction and exchange of information, ideas and experiences among members. In particular, within such a community, the preservation of knowledge is related to the role of older people, who transfer the knowledge and skills needed for their ancient working practices to the current generation.

Other scholars have focused on different indigenous and local communities, such as aboriginal (Australian) and BaNtwane (South African) people, showing how they can adopt the common goals that are shared by the whole community and can develop a set of practices within social relationships built up over time (e.g., Kelly and Gordon 2002; Smith et al. 2011). People of these communities feel a particular need to preserve culturally unique knowledge for future generations. The interaction among community members, arising from spending time together, sharing information, exploring ideas, and helping each other to solve problems, enables them to develop a set of knowledge that must be preserved over time. In this regard, as it has been done in the past, the best way to preserve knowledge is by practice. In cultivating community practices, members obtain two results: (a) getting tacit and explicit knowledge, and (b) preserving such knowledge over time. In this regard, social interaction is crucial for CoPs where collective learning keeps alive the practices developed in the past.

Again, other empirical evidence of CoPs may be traced back in time. Among the first knowledge-based social structures—the corporations in ancient Rome and the artisans in the Middle Ages, as shown by Lave and Wenger (1991)—and also the physicians, nurses, priests and nuns in the late Middle Ages and afterwards, are examples of communities where knowledge has been preserved through practice over time. Organizational literature, and research based on the social learning theory in particular, stresses the relationship between learning and the organizational context in which learning takes place, showing how context can determine the ways knowledge is transferred and preserved. In this regard, as shown by Mazour (2006), community of practice is a key tool for preserving collective knowledge because it is based on interaction and exchange among members who are recognized as repositories of knowledge.

Building upon academic literature and empirical evidence, in this study the concept of the knowledge preservation community is used to refer to the process of maintaining knowledge crucial to a CoP by storing knowledge and activities over time and providing members with the possibility of recall for the future.

In the next paragraphs, I will try to emphasize the interplay between practice and knowledge by providing an overview of the main research based on the practice-based approach to understanding the phenomenon of knowledge preservation. Then I will go on to identify the main mechanisms and tools enabling the preservation of explicit and tacit knowledge within a CoP.

3.2   A Practice-Based Approach to Community of Knowledge Preservation

Defining practice is not a simple task. Although with reference to community of practice the term "practice" has been used by various scholars in different ways, one of the most frequently used definitions of the concept of practice in a community is that provided by Wenger et al. (2002). According to these authors, practice refers to a shared repertoire of resources that includes experiences, stories, tools and ways of addressing recurring problems. In this regard, as explained previously, practice is "a sort of mini-culture that binds the community together" (Wenger et al. 2002, p. 39).

More generally, as recognized by the literature, the concept of practice draws from different intellectual backgrounds and, thus, is wider, deeper and more ambiguous than Wenger has in mind (e.g., Knorr Cetina 1997, 1999; Corradi et al. 2010). In effect, the concept of practice is stressed by certain scholars, who try to trace the similarities and differences in definitions and meanings (e.g., Cook and Brown 1999; Gherardi 2000; Carlile 2002; Nicolini et al. 2003; Corradi et al. 2010).

Corradi et al. (2010) provide a useful literature review on the concept of practice and trace the similarities in the definitions by distinguishing practices along two lines: as an "empirical object"—the locus in which scholars study the activities of the practitioners—and as "a way of seeing"—a more explicit acknowledgment of practice as epistemology. They identify the conceptual labels for each division. I have discussed the conceptual definitions of practice (labels) in Sect. 2.3.3, "*Practice*". Among the different definitions of practice reviewed by Corradi and colleagues, I focus on practice as a "way of seeing", and on the practice-based approach (e.g., Carlile 2002; Nicolini et al. 2003) in particular, in explaining knowledge preservation within CoPs.

Specifically, (Nicolini et al. 2003), in the book entitled *Knowing in Organizations: A Practice-based Approach*, outline a brief and interesting reconstruction of the notion of practice based on three cultural roots: Marx's work; phenomenology and symbolic interactionism; and Wittgenstein's legacy. Practice is crucial to Marx. According to him, thinking is only one of the things people do. Marx's studies focus on the praxis, understood as what people say, imagine, and think about concerning their activities. Although this view seems to focus more on what people do rather than what they are, Marx also explores the social dimension of practice. Indeed, according to Marx, people are producers and their output involves both the production of goods and the reproduction of society. From Marx to Wittgenstein, via phenomenology and symbolic interactionism, the concept of practice increasingly takes on a social and cultural meaning (Nicolini et al. 2003). This standpoint is also stressed by Wenger (1998), who adopts a symbolic-interactionist perspective for explaining the social dimension of practice within a community. He states that practice within a community is always social practice, understood as "doing in a historical and social context that gives structure and meaning to what we do" (Wenger 1998, p. 47). The community is also a place that allows people to interact with each other in developing new practices and adapting old ones. Indeed, as Wenger et al. (2002) argue, practice evolves within a community as a "collective product" arising from the exchange of information found in documents, articles, books, websites and other repositories, as well as from observing and experimenting with new ways to perform a task. In this regard, practice has been defined as "a sort of mini-culture that binds the community together" (Wenger et al. 2002, p. 39).

Nicolini et al. (2003) also develop a "practice-based vocabulary" aimed at providing a theoretical repertoire on the notion of practice and practice-based knowing and learning. The authors identify certain characteristics of this vocabulary, of which the most important are: (a) the presence of verbs often taking the form of the gerund (e.g., doing, being, etc.), of which the most frequently used are learning, organizing, belonging, understanding, translating and knowing; (b) the predominance of socially related terms that emphasize the social dimension of knowing, often focusing on the situated nature of knowledge; (c) the presence of terms referring to material and symbolic artifacts, highlighting that sociality exists not only with other human beings, but also with artifacts. In this regard, the practice-based approach does not view knowledge as mental content, but as a factor of organizational life that may be enacted and reproduced in practice. Practice is a key to the comprehension of knowledge-related phenomena, while knowledge is the "practice that institutionalized, historically determined, and codified expertise acquires sense and becomes both a resource and a constraint for action" (Nicolini et al. 2003, p. 26). Thus, the practice-based approach is a lens to the study of knowing and learning in organizations that offers a newer ontology and epistemology than previous ones have offered (Nicolini et al. 2003).

Besides Nicolini et al. (2003), other scholars also focus on practice and, in particular, on the link between knowledge and practice, by using the practice-based approach for explaining how people construct their competence in practice (e.g., Carlile 1997, 2002). Building on the research of Lave and Wenger (1991), Brown and Duguid (1991), Orr (1996), such studies look at the situated nature of knowledge. In particular, linking the literature on CoP and knowledge management, Carlile (2002) developed a pragmatic view of knowledge, acknowledging it as localized, embedded and invested in practice. According to the authors, if knowledge is localized, this does not mean it is limited to only one situation or location, but is localized around a similar set of problems faced in a given practice (Carlile 2002). Knowledge embedded in practice, instead, recalls Polanyi's concept of "tacit knowing" and refers to knowledge accumulated in the experiences and know-how of people engaged in a given practice. Finally, knowledge invested in practice refers to methods, ways of doing things, and successes that demonstrate the value of the knowledge developed. Using an anthropological approach, Carlile (2002, p. 446) explores knowledge across four CoPs, so observing that the "objects they work with and the ends that they pursue provides a concrete delineation of what to observe and what to compare in terms of how knowledge is created and structured." As a result, such research shows that knowledge is structured in practice and in "objects" (artifacts that individuals work with) and "ends" (outcomes that demonstrate success in creating, measuring, or manipulating objects) that are of consequence in a given practice (Carlile 2002).

Finally, based on the practice-based approach, other research focuses on practice for understanding the reasons leading people to join a community aimed at preserving knowledge rather than to create a new one (Schiavone and Agrifoglio 2012; Agrifoglio and Metallo 2015). Both studies stress the concept of practice, showing the crucial role of the CoP as a place for preserving practice (Schiavone and Agrifoglio 2012) and explicit and tacit knowledge (Agrifoglio and Metallo 2015). These studies look at the CoP as a place where members share and preserve knowledge not only by interaction and social exchange, but above all by cultivating community practice. Within such communities, older members who possess knowledge and skills useful for doing a work are constantly involved in all community initiatives and activities and play an active role in the knowledge preservation process. As Agrifoglio and Metallo (2015, p. 107) suggested, "knowledge is also embedded in the stories of people and in their working experiences. [...] Community of practice is an efficient tool for helping people internalize knowledge because it allows them to talk about their experiences and to exchange knowledge while working on a specific problem." In this regard, CoP has been recognized as a tool for preserving knowledge because, as Carlile (2002) suggested, such knowledge is localized, embedded and invested in practice.

3.3 Preserving Knowledge in the Community of Practice

As explained before, the preservation of knowledge is a particular phase in the process of knowledge management for organizations. Knowledge preservation allows us to select, store, and actualize knowledge and experience arising from a specific context. Although existing academic debate mainly focuses on different forms of knowledge, such as tacit and explicit or individual and collective, and on the knowledge management process, such as the transforming process of such knowledge (codification and transfer inside and outside the organization), preserving knowledge is equally important because it enables organizations to avoid knowledge loss (e.g., corporate memory). When losses occur, organizations can replace what is lost through high investment in creating this knowledge or obtaining it from outside (Davidavičienė and Raudeliūnienė 2010).

Some scholars (e.g., Ardichvili et al. 2003; Lazaric et al. 2003; Amin and Roberts 2008; Fang and Chiu 2010; Agrifoglio and Metallo 2015) link knowledge management literature and CoP research by focusing on the role of knowledge within communities as well as on the process leading to the creation, transfer and storage of knowledge itself. However, although CoP is widely recognized by organizational research and IS literature as an efficient tool for knowledge generation and sharing (e.g., Wenger 1998; Ardichvili et al. 2003, 2006; Wasko and Faraj 2005; Fang and Chiu 2010), few scholars recognize it as a natural and ideal context for selecting and storing knowledge and technical skills about a particular technology, as well as for exploiting them to create new ones (e.g., Lazaric et al. 2003; Amin and Roberts 2008; Schiavone and Agrifoglio 2012; Agrifoglio and Metallo 2015). Among them, the research of Lazaric et al. (2003), Schiavone and Agrifoglio (2012) mainly focuses on tacit knowledge preservation within CoPs. On the other hand, the research of Agrifoglio and Metallo (2015) focuses on explicit and tacit knowledge preservation within CoPs. Finally, Amin and Roberts (2008) explore the reciprocal interplay between explicit and tacit knowledge and knowing (knowing as action).

This paragraph brings together knowledge management literature and CoP research in order to investigate how communities preserve knowledge over time. In particular, I will explain further below the main mechanisms used by CoPs for preserving different forms of knowledge, such as explicit and tacit, and will show the contribution of "knowing" toward this process.

Organizational studies view the different forms of knowledge—such as explicit and tacit, individual and collective, or know-how and know-that—as constituting the focus of what they call "the epistemology of possession" (Cook and Brown 1999). Based on this perspective, knowledge is something that people possess in their heads, which enables them to perform an action. According to Polanyi (1966), people are able to ride a bicycle if they know how to stay upright and how to turn the handlebars to prevent a fall. Thus, riding a bicycle requires that people possess both explicit and tacit knowledge for performing such behavior. In this regard, knowledge is not the activity of riding itself, but it is something used in riding.

However, knowledge does not capture all of what is known. Cook and Brown (1999), indeed, distinguish "what is known" (knowledge) from "what is part of action" (knowing). Knowing "is not something that is used or necessary to action, but rather something that is a part of action […] Knowing is that aspect of action (or practice) that does epistemic work" (Cook and Brown 1999, p. 387). In a broader sense, knowing has also been recognized as the product of interaction with the social and physical world. In this sense, what people know (knowledge) and what people do (knowing) are the products of ongoing concrete interaction between them and the social and physical context or circumstance at a given time (y Gasset 1961; Cook and Brown 1999). Cook and Brown (1999) view knowing as constituting the focus of what they call "the epistemology of practice."

These two epistemologies—possession and practice—are not only related to each other, but are complementary and mutually enabling. In fact, because on the one hand knowledge is a tool of knowing, while on the other hand it means the interplay between knowledge and knowing, this enables the creation of new knowledge and ways of knowing (Cook and Brown 1999). Building upon the Cook and Brown (1999) theoretical model, I will look more precisely at knowledge and knowing, and the link between them, with particular reference to the process of knowledge preservation: –the selection, storage and actualization of knowledge within CoPs. Figure 3.1 shows the relationships between knowledge and knowing within a CoP.

In respect of the framework of Cook and Brown (1999), this chapter does not split knowledge into individual and collective because this distinction is less suitable for CoPs. As the literature on CoP states (e.g., Hutchins 1995; Duguid 2005): within communities, knowledge, in explicit and tacit form, is distributed across collectivity and their artifacts rather than held by or divisible among individuals (Hutchins 1995; Duguid 2005).

Furthermore, based on the Cook and Brown (1999), Duguid (2005) research, this chapter will show the mechanisms and technologies for preserving explicit and tacit knowledge within a CoP, without considering interplay among those two forms. In the past, explicit and tacit knowledge have been viewed as two unified, but alternative, dimensions along the ongoing continuum of knowledge. However, like all the dimensions on a continuum, explicit and tacit knowledge are distinct at two ends of the continuum. On the contrary, they are also recognized as two different and complementary forms of knowledge (e.g. Polanyi 1966; Cook and Brown 1999; Duguid 2005). According to Ryle (1949), knowing how and knowing that are two complementary aspects of knowing. However, although knowing how helps to make knowing that actionable, they are not substitutable. Similarly, Polanyi (1966) shows that tacit knowledge is not reducible to the explicit form. The accumulation of tacit knowledge, indeed, does not lead to explicit knowledge. This perspective is enhanced by Duguid (2005), who stresses the problems related to knowledge codification and articulation from one form to the other.

As explained above, indeed, people are able to ride a bicycle if they possess both forms of knowledge. People who possess only explicit knowledge are not able to stay upright, while people who possess only tacit knowledge do not know where to turn the handlebars. At the same time, explicit and tacit knowledge are not substitutable (Cook and Brown 1999; Duguid 2005). Unlike the Nonaka (1991, 1994) research, these studies show that explicit knowledge cannot be converted into tacit

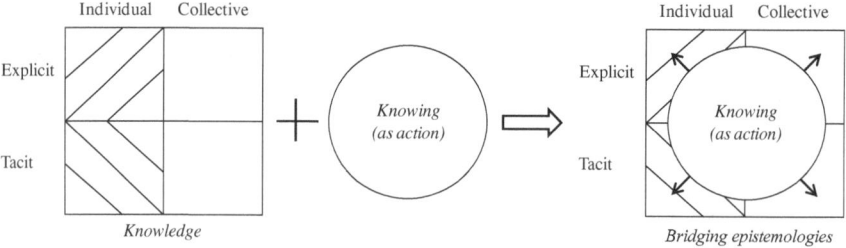

Fig. 3.1 Knowledge and knowing within a CoP. *Source* adapted from Cook and Brown 1999

knowledge and, on the other hand, tacit knowledge cannot be turned into explicit. However, each of these forms of knowledge can be used as an aid in acquiring the other. More specifically, "explicit knowledge can be used as an aid to help acquire the tacit knowledge, but cannot by itself enable one to ride. The tacit knowledge is necessary in being able to ride, but it does not by itself enable a rider to say which way to turn" (Cook and Brown 1999, p. 385). In this regard, explicit and tacit knowledge, thus, are viewed as two different and nonconvertible forms of knowledge that community members possess and which enable them to perform a specific practice.

Thus, in what follows, using the distinction between the epistemology of possession (forms of knowledge) and the epistemology of practice (knowing), I will explore the mechanisms and tools enabling CoPs to preserve the collective forms of explicit and tacit knowledge.

3.3.1 Mechanisms and Tools for Preserving Explicit Knowledge

Building upon the research of Ryle (1949), Polanyi (1966) distinguished knowledge into two dimensions: explicit and tacit. Explicit knowledge, well-known as codified knowledge, is a kind of knowledge transmittable in a formal and systematic language. In respect of tacit knowledge, it is codified and communicated by symbolic and natural language and appears valuable (Nonaka 1994). Usually, explicit knowledge is expressed and recorded as words, numbers and codes. However, visual and sound notations could be also considered as other ways to codify knowledge. By its nature, this form of knowledge is easy to communicate, store and distribute.

The preservation of explicit knowledge within a CoP is less difficult than preserving tacit knowledge. Since explicit knowledge is codified, it can be easy to transfer within and outside organizational boundaries. Lam (2000) defined as "encoded knowledge" the collective form of explicit knowledge, sometimes referred to as information, that is conveyed by signs and symbols. It is a process that allows the abstraction of an individual's experiences and knowledge into more generic knowledge that is codified, transferred and stored through various mechanisms, such as physical, verbal and written communication and tools. Books, manuals, blueprints, spreadsheets and written documents in general, as well as lessons, workshops, storytelling and other verbal and physical communication, are examples of tools used for sharing and preserving explicit knowledge over time. Like any organization, a CoP is able to perform activities by using collective knowledge arising from inside and outside boundaries. Members usually collect explicit knowledge related to community practice from inside and outside community boundaries in order to share it with others (Agrifoglio and Metallo 2015). Beyond the source, within a community the possession of explicit knowledge, and thus its preservation, is a necessary condition for enabling members to perform a certain activity.

In agreement with previous literature, the mechanisms that enable a CoP to preserve the collective form of explicit knowledge are physical, verbal and written communication.

By its nature, explicit knowledge could be codified and transferred between people via physical and verbal communication both inside and outside an organizational context. People who understand issues and appreciate the evolution of their field could be more willing to update community knowledge by moving such explicit knowledge required for doing an activity from outside to inside organizational boundaries. At the same time, active participation by community members in community life also enables them to exchange explicit knowledge that would otherwise remain only in the minds of individuals. In this regard, the simple exchange of "know-what"—i.e., information, knowledge and facts—among community members allows them to preserve and then to exploit that knowledge in working practice. For instance, community members usually get explicit knowledge through attending conferences, seminars and events and then reporting back to the others. In the same way, storytelling has been recognized as an important tool of communication allowing community members to preserve know-what through the narration of their life and work experiences. In this regard, knowledge sharing is also a way for preserving explicit knowledge.

Furthermore, explicit knowledge may be easily codified and preserved trough the mechanism of written communication. Writing has always been one of the most effective mechanisms to preserve and transfer explicit knowledge through signs and symbols. Within communities, written communication has allowed people to pass knowledge needed for a specific practice across generations over time. For instance, academic research on heritage shows that stones, papyrus and books are examples of a wide range of ancient tools, based on the mechanism of written communication, used to transfer and store knowledge within a community. Books, manuals, reports, etc. are examples of more recent tools used for preserving explicit knowledge, as well as for transferring knowledge within and across community boundaries. Currently, face-to-face CoPs are increasingly replaced by virtual communities, whose members use ICT for communicating among themselves and for managing knowledge. Thanks to ICT, written communication tools used for preserving knowledge are now also available in digital form. Virtual CoPs use ICT, such as web 2.0 and team collaboration tools, to enable members to communicate and share information with each other, as well as to select and store knowledge; for example, on databases, web-based access to data, data mining and web portals (Davidavičienė and Raudeliūnienė 2010). Empirical evidence, indeed, shows not only the crucial role of CoP in knowledge creation and sharing, but also its contribution to explicit knowledge preservation within organizational boundaries. However, as Wenger et al. claimed (2002, p. 9), "not everything we know can be codified as documents and tolls," implying that often individuals and communities preserve knowledge in explicit ways, so emphasizing the tacit form of knowledge.

3.3.2 Mechanisms and Tools for Preserving Tacit Knowledge

The term tacit knowledge, often called implicit knowledge, was first introduced into social science by Michael Polanyi in 1958. As Polanyi put it at that time, "We can know more than we can tell" (Polanyi 1966, p. 4). In fact, knowledge is not only something that can be expressed in words and numbers, but is also deeply rooted in action, commitment and the involvement of individuals (Nonaka 1994). Polanyi's distinction between tacit and explicit knowledge recalls Gilbert Ryle's (1949) "knowing how/knowing that" distinction. In particular, knowing that something is the case is a matter of having a disposition or "capacity to," while knowing how is a disposition to a set of behaviors or "capacity for" (Fantl 2008). In this regard, knowing that refers to codified information that could be acquired in explicit form, while knowing how refers to information that people can acquire by practice.

Unlike explicit knowledge, tacit knowledge is defined as something that it is revealed through application and cannot be written down. According to Polanyi (1974), it "indwells" in comprehensive cognizance of the human mind and body. With reference to the example of riding a bicycle, Polanyi (1962, p. 1) states that "I can say that I know how to ride a bicycle or how to swim, but this does not mean that I can tell how I manage to keep my balance on a bicycle or keep afloat when swimming. I know how to carry out these performances as a whole and that I also know how to carry out the elementary acts which constitute them, but that, though I know these acts, I cannot tell what they are." In this regard, "what I can say" is the explicit dimension of knowledge, while "what is known for" keeping upright on a bicycle is definable as the tacit dimension.

Although the literature agrees about the concept of tacit knowledge, the possibility of articulating (transforming) tacit knowledge into explicit knowledge has no such convergence of views (Håkanson 2003). In particular, some scholars view tacit knowledge as knowledge that cannot be articulated (e.g., Grant and Baden-Fuller 1995). Others view tacit knowledge as knowledge that is difficult, if not impossible, to articulate (e.g., Berman et al. 2002). "It is possible to convert some tacit knowledge into explicit knowledge […] but much tacit knowledge is difficult, if not impossible, to codify and can never be made explicit" (Berman et al. 2002, p. 14). On the contrary, other writers do not exclude the possibility of articulating tacit into explicit knowledge (e.g., Grant 1996; Nonaka 1994). According to this perspective, as Grant (1996) suggested, knowing how can be codified into explicit knowledge about facts and theory. Nonaka (1994, p. 18) echoed this perspective, assuming that "knowledge is created through conversion between tacit and explicit knowledge." Other scholars, instead, argue that tacit knowledge could be an aid to acquiring explicit knowledge, although the two forms of knowledge are not articulable in terms of each other (e.g., Ryle 1949; Polanyi 1966; Cook and Brown 1999; Duguid 2005). According to such research, tacit forms of knowledge help to make explicit forms actionable and vice versa, but neither can be converted into the other (Cook and Brown 1999).

Some scholars link knowledge management literature and CoP research by focusing on the mechanisms and/or technologies enabling a community to preserve tacit knowledge (Lazaric et al. 2003; Schiavone and Agrifoglio 2012; Agrifoglio and Metallo 2015).

Lazaric et al. (2003) view explicit (scientific) and empirical (tacit) dimensions as two forms of knowledge that can be articulated and codified and thus shared among community members at different levels. However, as the authors recognize, knowledge, and its tacit form in particular, cannot always be articulated, so that it is made explicit by means of language and transferred between community members. "Although some forms of knowledge can benefit from it (the process of articulation of knowledge), parts of tacit knowledge may defy articulation and be poorly reproduced and communicated. In other words, only a small fraction of articulable knowledge can in fact be articulated" (Lazaric et al. 2003, p. 1833). Thus, although the study highlights the difficulty of articulating tacit knowledge, it does not exclude the possibility. Besides the process of tacit knowledge articulation, this study also investigates how organizations preserve tacit knowledge over time. In particular, based on empirical evidence of CoPs in the French steel industry, it focuses on the main mechanisms and tools enabling people to preserve tacit knowledge. The starting point is that organizations are a special context in which tacit knowledge is selected by social and relational interaction among people and then stored in organizational routines (Nelson and Winter 1982). In this regard, the social and relational context is the mechanism that enables the preservation of collective forms of tacit knowledge, while organizational routines, such as different kinds of equipment, tools, procedures, data, human know-how, etc., are the tools used in such preservation. Building upon Nelson and Winter's (1982) concept of "routinized" organization, the authors remark that the performance of a practice arises from compliance with procedures and rules embedding collective know-how and knowledge existing within a community. Within communities, the social and relational context in which routines are activated leads to institutionalization of the tacit knowledge needed for doing an action through the articulation of best practices from individuals to the whole organization.

Similarly, Agrifoglio and Metallo (2015) also stress the role of the social and relational context as a mechanism for preserving tacit knowledge within a community of practice. Since tacit knowledge is embedded in people's stories and their working experiences, a CoP is an ideal place for helping members to internalize tacit knowledge by specific mechanisms such as observation "of" and performance of working practice "with." Based on this point of view, a CoP is thus recognized as a natural place for preserving and sharing the collective form of tacit knowledge through social and relational dynamics that help members to perform a specific practice (Agrifoglio and Metallo 2015). However, this study notes the possibility of preserving tacit knowledge through the mechanism of social context, while it detects no tools for doing so.

Schiavone and Agrifoglio (2012), instead, identify practice as the main mechanism for preserving tacit knowledge. In particular, they assume that carrying out a specific practice enables people to institutionalize (store and capitalize) know-that and know-how about artifacts that otherwise might be lost over time. Building upon Marx's research, practice is viewed as a system of activities in which knowing is not separable from doing, and learning is a social and not merely a cognitive activity. Within a CoP, members interact with each other to perform a specific practice, so accumulating the tacit knowledge needed to do it better. In this regard, community members create, store and transfer know-how collectively through their practice. Thus, the preservation of a practice also enables community members to preserve the tacit knowledge required for doing so (Schiavone and Agrifoglio 2012).

Building on previous research, the main mechanisms for preserving tacit knowledge are social and relational context and practice, while the tools are related to shared repertoire. As explained previously, shared repertoire concerns the common resources, such as routines, sensibilities, artifacts, stories, vocabulary, styles, etc., that members use to negotiate meaning and facilitate learning within a community (Wenger 1998). According to Lam (2000), Brown and Duguid (2001), the collective form of tacit knowledge resides in organizational routines and shared norms and is rooted within a CoP because it is socially constructed. Community of practice is thus viewed as a place of social exchange, where a collective form of tacit knowledge is embedded within a shared repertoire that is socially constructed and activated by its members through carrying out a practice. In this regard, shared repertoire, in which tacit knowledge resides, enables community members to perform a practice, while the carrying out of such practice allows them to structure it through a process of knowledge sharing and preservation.

In agreement with Cook and Brown's (1999) framework, this study posits that the social and relational dimension is a mechanism that concerns knowing as action rather than knowledge as possession, and therefore it indirectly contributes to preserving knowledge through practice. However, this point is particularly evident in explicit knowledge, where knowing helps to preserve such knowledge, but is not the primary mechanism. On the contrary, the preservation of collective forms of tacit knowledge seems to arise from different mechanisms than knowing. The interplay between tacit knowledge and knowing, as well as the contribution of knowing to knowledge preservation, will be better explained in the next paragraph.

3.3.3 Adding Knowing to Knowledge Preservation

As explained above, with the term "knowing" I refer to the epistemological dimension of action itself (Cook and Brown 1999). Knowing is not something necessary to action or something that is used in action, but rather something that is a part of action. Riding a bicycle, playing the piano, working with wood, driving a car, etc., are some examples of daily actions in which knowledge, both explicit and tacit, is necessary for the epistemology of possession and knowing is work done as part of action itself (or practice): epistemology of practice.

In order to better understand the meaning of knowing, it is useful to distinguish the term "practice" from "action" and "behavior." In particular, while behavior is what people do, action is a behavior imbued with meaning—intentional, purposeful, and conscious. For example, riding a bicycle is a behavior, while riding a bicycle to go home is an action. In the latter case, the behavior has a meaning because it is useful for achieving a goal. Practice, instead, refers to "the coordinated activities of individuals or groups in doing their 'real work' as it is informed by a particular organizational or group context" (Cook and Brown 1999, pp. 386–387). More simply, it is what people do at work by drawing information from an organizational context of which they themselves are an integral part. Thus, a professional cyclist who rides a bicycle, and a mechanic who tests a bicycle after repair, etc., are examples of practice rather than of action or behavior. This is because they are part of a context that has its own collective knowledge, which they draw on and contribute to with their work. In this regard, practice is not only what people do within a specific context, but is also the locus for the production and reproduction of social relations.

CoPs are recognized as a natural setting where social relations enable members to perform a set of coordinated activities necessary for doing a task. Within communities, it is possible to distinguish knowledge (what we know) and knowing (what we do), as well as the interplay between them. With reference to interplay between knowledge and knowing, Cook and Brown (1999, p. 393) assume that "Knowing does not sit statically on top of knowledge. Quite the contrary, since knowing is an aspect of our interaction with the world, its relationship with knowledge is dynamic. Each of the forms of knowledge is brought into play by knowing when knowledge is used as a tool in interaction with the world. Knowledge, meanwhile, gives shape and discipline to knowing." Thus, while knowledge enables members to perform a practice, it is also constructed by practicing in a context of interaction (Gherardi 2000). Practice in a context is a way to enable people to acquire knowledge (Cook and Brown 1999; Gherardi 2000; Orlikowski 2002; Nicolini et al. 2003).

Unlike Cook and Brown (1999), Orlikowski (2002) outlines a perspective on knowing in practice in distributed organizations based on the different assumption that tacit knowledge is a form of knowing. In this regard, she states that tacit knowledge is not distinct and separable from knowing and thus from action, because it is constituted through such action. Building upon this perspective, knowing is viewed as a complement to "the existing perspectives on knowledge by insisting on the essential role of human agency in accomplishing knowledgeable work" (Orlikowski 2002, p. 269). Thus, knowing is constituted every day in the ongoing and situated practice of community members. It is socially constituted and thus collected and distributed within the organizational boundaries of a community, even if its members are geographically dispersed.

Thus, although Cook and Brown (1999), Orlikowski (2002) view the interplay between tacit knowledge and knowing in different ways, their findings move in the same direction by highlighting the contribution of social relations in sharing knowing how within rather than across the context of organizations where people work. However, knowing how and knowing that must also be seen as a starting point, over the concept of arrival. As Cook and Brown (1999, p. 397) assume, the "production of new knowledge does not lie in a continuous interaction between tacit and explicit knowledge but rather in our interaction with the world. Specifically, it lies in the use of knowledge (explicit and/or tacit) as tools of productive inquiry (of the sort we have called 'knowing') as part of our dynamic interaction with the things of the social and physical world." In this regard, knowledge is a necessary condition for action, and the latter is crucial for acquiring and sharing knowledge itself. Thus, distinguishing between the epistemology of possession and the epistemology of practice could be particularly useful in helping us to understand the interplay between "what people know" and "what people do" within the setting of an organization where they are engaged.

Similarly, within a CoP, collective knowledge draws on the context of where people are and what they contribute to, and enables people to carry out an action. Such action also aids people to transfer already acquired knowledge and to develop new forms of it. For instance, within a community of physicians, explicit and tacit forms of knowledge enable the doctors to understand the patients' symptoms and thus to make a medical diagnosis. At the same time, doing such action (practice) enables the physicians to help each other in order to make the diagnosis as effectively as possible and to prescribe the most appropriate care. By carrying out a practice, indeed, community members use the explicit and tacit knowledge necessary for knowing. Also, the latter enables them to expand knowledge through a mutual and recursive process. Building on Giddens (1979, 1984), within a CoP members draw upon "structure" (known as shared repertoire such as organizational routines, shared norms, artifacts, vocabulary, etc.) to perform social actions through practice, while structure is also the result of these social practices. Structure is both the medium and the outcome of the reproduction of practices. In this regard, structuration could be viewed as a process that enables communities to develop, share and store knowledge through practice. Within communities, indeed, both explicit and tacit knowledge enables knowing, and the latter allows members to structure such knowledge by carrying out a specific practice in the context of interaction.

3.4   Toward a Dynamic Framework for Community Knowledge Preservation

This chapter aims to explore the topic of knowledge preservation within CoPs. After reviewing the managerial literature on knowledge management, and knowledge preservation in particular, and IS research on community of practice, it first provides a conceptualization of the "knowledge preservation community"; that is, the process for maintaining knowledge crucial to a CoP, which stores knowledge and activities over time and offers its members the possibility of recall in the future.

Furthermore, in respect of previous research on knowledge preservation, this study offers a different and deeper perspective for understanding the phenomenon by exploring the mechanisms and tools enabling a CoP to select, store and actualize the collective form of explicit and tacit knowledge. Building upon Cook and Brown (1999), this research distinguishes knowledge (epistemology of possession) and knowing (epistemology of practice) in understanding the mechanisms and tools enabling CoPs to preserve the collective ontological dimension—rather than individual forms—of tacit and explicit knowledge. As managerial literature suggests (e.g., Davidavičienė and Raudeliūnienė 2010), knowledge preservation tools are crucial in facing some of the biggest organizational challenges, such as avoiding the loss of knowledge (amnesia). Indeed, knowledge that is anchored only in the heads of the employees, rather than institutionalized within the organization, is a strong threat for a firm, due to the failure to transfer such knowledge from individual to collective memory.

Finally, it has also explored the interplay between knowledge and knowing, rather than the articulation of explicit into tacit forms and vice versa, showing the contribution of practice in preserving knowledge. As explained above, practice in a social context, and in a community of practice in particular, comes from and contributes to knowledge, thanks to the interaction that community members have with the world. In this regard, the relationship between knowledge and knowing is reciprocal and dynamic. While knowledge is seen as abstract and static, knowing is concrete and dynamic. Thus, adding knowing to knowledge contributes to building a dynamic model of analysis that allows us to explore the preservation of knowledge within a CoP focusing on knowledge and knowing, as well as on the interplay between them. Bringing together knowledge and knowing, this study has tried to clarify how and where the collective forms of tacit and explicit knowledge are respectively encoded or embedded. Figure 3.2 offers an overview of the main mechanisms and tools enabling knowledge preservation within a CoP.

As Fig. 3.2 shows, the collective form of explicit knowledge can be preserved by three mechanisms—written, verbal and physical communication—and in various tools that can be distinguished as traditional and digital tools. Traditional tools are usually used in face-to-face communities and allow members to preserve and transfer explicit knowledge within and across organizational boundaries. On the contrary, digital tools are usually used in virtual communities because they allow dispersed members to communicate among themselves and to preserve and transfer explicit knowledge without spatial and temporal limits. In respect of traditional tools, these allow more efficient communication, even if less rich, and have much greater storage capacity. Furthermore, knowing also contributes to collective forms of explicit knowledge preservation. Within a CoP, the interplay between knowledge and knowing is dynamic. Indeed, while explicit knowledge enables members to perform a practice, it is also constructed by practicing in a context of interaction (Gherardi 2000). Practice encourages written, verbal and physical communication among community members, so contributing to the preservation of explicit knowledge by using different traditional and digital tools.

Community/ Knowledge	Mechanisms	Tools
Explicit Knowledge	Written, verbal and physical communication	*Traditional tools*: Books, manuals, reports, etc. Lessons, workshop, storytelling, etc. *IT assisted tools*: Knowledge Management Systems Database Data Warehouse and data mining Web portals e-mail Videoconferencing
Tacit Knowledge	Practice in social context	Shared repertoire (routines, shared norms, artifacts, vocabulary, etc.)

Knowing (as action)

Fig. 3.2 Mechanisms and tools for preserving knowledge

Furthermore, Fig. 3.2 also shows the mechanisms and tools enabling CoPs to preserve collective forms of tacit knowledge. In respect of explicit knowledge, the preservation of tacit knowledge is maintained only through knowing. Since tacit knowledge is (by its nature) something that is revealed through application and cannot be written down, mechanisms enabling its direct preservation are not revealed. Based on Cook and Brown's (1999) research, this study differs from the body of research in assuming that tacit knowledge is a form of knowing. Tacit knowledge is viewed as something required for knowing, but it is not knowing itself. In the same way, knowing leads toward the structuration of tacit knowledge into organization. Within a community, tacit knowledge is embedded into shared repertoire, enabling community members to perform a practice. The latter also allows a community to institutionalize—store and capitalize—such knowledge into shared repertoire that is socially constructed.

References

Agrifoglio, R., & Metallo, C. (2015). Preserving knowledge through community of practice: A multiple case study. In L. Mola, F. Pennarola & S. Za (Eds.), *From information to smart society* (Vol. 5, pp. 103–111). Lecture Notes in Information Systems and Organisation (LNISO), Springer.

Amin, A., & Roberts, J. (2008). Knowing in action: Beyond communities of practice. *Research Policy, 37*, 353–369.

Anand, V., Glick, W. H., & Manz, C. C. (2002). Thriving on the knowledge of outsiders: Tapping organizational social capital. *The Academy of Management Executive, 16*(1), 87–101.

Ardichvili, A., Maurer, M., Li, W., Wentling, T., & Stuedemann, R. (2006). Cultural influences on knowledge sharing through online communities of practice. *Journal of Knowledge Management, 10*(1), 94–107.

Ardichvili, A., Page, V., & Wentling, T. (2003). Motivation and barriers to participation in virtual knowledge-sharing communities of practice. *Journal of Knowledge Management, 7*(1), 64–77.

Berman, S. L., Down, J., & Hill, C. W. L. (2002). Tacit knowledge as a source of competitive advantage in the national basketball association. *Academy of Management Journal, 45*(1), 13–23.

Brown, J. S., & Duguid, P. (1991). Organizational learning and communities-of-practice: Toward a unified view of working, learning, and innovation. *Organization Science, 2*(1), 40–57.

Brown, J. S., & Duguid, P. (2000). Mysteries of the region: Knowledge dynamics. In C. M. Lee (Ed.), *A habitat for innovation and entrepreneurship* (pp. 16–39). Santa Clara County: Stanford University Press.

Brown, J. S., & Duguid, P. (2001). Knowledge and organization: A social-practice perspective. *Organization Science, 12*(2), 198–213.

Carlile, P. (1997). *Transforming knowledge in product development: Making knowledge manifest through boundary objects*. Unpublished dissertation, University of Michigan, Ann Arbor, MI.

Carlile, P. R. (2002). A pragmatic view of knowledge and boundaries: Boundary objects in new product development. *Organization Science, 13*(4), 442–455.

Cook, S. D. N., & Brown, J. S. (1999). Bridging epistemologies: The generative dance between organizational knowledge and organizational knowing. *Organization Science, 10*(4), 381–400.

Corradi, G., Gherardi, S., & Verzelloni, L. (2010). Through the practice lens: Where is the bandwagon of practice-based studies heading? *Management Learning, 41*(3), 265–283.

Davidavičienė, V., & Raudeliūnienė, J. (2010). ICT in tacit knowledge preservation. In *The 6th International Scientific Conference "Business and Management 2010"* (pp. 436–442), May 13–14, 2010, Vilnius, Lithuania.

Duguid, P. (2005). The art of knowing: Social and tacit dimensions of knowledge and the limits of the community of practice. *The Information Society, 21*(2), 109–118.

Fang, Y. H., & Chiu, C. M. (2010). In justice we trust: Exploring Knowledge-sharing continuance intentions in virtual communities of practice. *Computers in Human Behavior, 26*(2), 235–246.

Fantl, J. (2008). Knowing-how and knowing-that. *Philosophy Compass, 3*(3), 451–470.

Gherardi, S. (2000). Practice-based theorizing on learning and knowing in organizations: An introduction. *Organization, 7*(2), 211–223.

Giddens, A. (1979). *Central problems in social theory: Action, structure, and contradiction in social analysis*. California: University of California Press.

Giddens, A. (1984). *The constitution of society: Outline of a theory of structuration*. Cambridge: Polity Press.

Grant, R. M. (1996). Towards a knowledge-based view of the firm. *Strategic Management Journal, 17*(Winter Special Issue), 109–122.

Grant, R. M., & Baden-Fuller, C. (1995). A knowledge-based theory of inter-firm collaboration. In *Academy of management proceedings* (Vol. 1, pp. 17–21). Academy of management. http://proceedings.aom.org/content/1995/1/17.full.pdf+html. Accessed February 10, 2015.

Håkansson, L. (2003). Creating knowledge the power and logic of articulation. In *Academy of management meeting*. Seattle: Academy of Management.

Hutchins, E. (1995). *Cognition in the wild*. Cambridge: MIT press.

Kelly, L., & Gordon, P. (2002). Developing a community of practice: Museums and reconciliation in Australia. In R. Sandell (Ed.), *Museums, society, inequality* (pp. 173–174). London and New York: Routledge.

Knorr Cetina, K. (1997). Sociality with objects. Social relations in postsocial knowledge societies. *Theory, Culture & Society, 14*(4), 1–30.

Knorr Cetina, K. (1999). *Financial markets and the cultural production of transparency*. Paper presented at the Annual Meeting of the American Sociological Association, Chicago, 6–10 August, 1999.

Lam, A. (2000). Tacit knowledge, organizational learning and societal institutions: An integrated framework. *Organization studies, 21*(3), 487–513.

Lave, J., & Wenger, E. (1991). *Situated learning: Legitimate peripheral participation*. Cambridge: Cambridge University Press.

Lazaric, N., Mangolte, P. A., & Massué, M. L. (2003). Articulation and codification of collective know-how in the steel industry: Evidence from blast furnace control in France. *Research Policy, 32*(10), 1829–1847.

Malhotra, Y. (2005). Integrating knowledge management technologies in organizational business processes: Getting real time enterprises to deliver real business performance. *Journal of knowledge management, 9*(1), 7–28.

Mazour, T. (2006). Knowledge preservation and transfer: issues and terminology. In *Proceedings of School of Nuclear Knowledge Management*, September 18–22, 2006. http://indico.ictp.it/event/a05221/session/13/contribution/8/material/0/0.pdf. Accessed February 18, 2015.

Miller, D., & Shamsie, J. (1996). The resource-based view of the firm in two environments: The Hollywood firm studios from 1936 to 1965. *Academy of Management Journal, 39*(3), 519–543.

Nelson, R. R., & Winter, S. G. (1982). *An evolutionary theory of economic change*. Cambridge: Harvard University Press.

Nicolini, D., Gherardi, S., & Yanow, D. (2003). *Knowing in organizations: A practice-based approach*. USA: M. E. Sharpe Inc.

Nonaka, I. (1991). The knowledge-creating company. *Harvard Business Review, 69*, 96–104.

Nonaka, I. (1994). *A dynamic theory of organizational knowledge creation*. Kunitachi, Tokyo: Institute of Business Research. Hitotsubashi University.

Orlikowski, W. J. (2002). Knowing in practice: Enacting a collective capability in distributed organizing. *Organization Science, 13*(3), 249–273.

Orr, J. E. (1996). *Talking about machines: An ethnography of a modern job*. Ithaca: Cornell University Press.

Polanyi, M. (1958). *Personal knowledge*. Chicago, IL: University of Chicago Press.

Polanyi, M. (1962). *Personal knowledge* (2nd ed.). Chicago, IL: University of Chicago Press.

Polanyi, M. (1966). *The tacit dimension*. New York, NY: Doubleday.

Polanyi, M. (1974). Scientific thought and social reality: Essays by Michael Polanyi. *Psychological Issues*.

Ryle, G. (1949). *The concept of mind*. London: Hutchinson.

Schiavone, F., & Agrifoglio, R. (2012). Communities of practice and practice preservation: A case study. In M. De Marco, D. Te'eni, V. Albano & S. Za, *Information systems: Crossroads for organization, management, accounting and engineering*. Berlin Heidelberg: Springer-verlag.

Smith, A., Reitsma, L., Van Den Hoven, E., Kotzé, P., & Coetzee, L. (2011). Towards preserving indigenous oral stories using tangible objects. In *Culture and computing (Culture Computing), 2011 Second International Conference on* (pp. 86–91), IEEE.

Wasko, M. M., & Faraj, S. (2005). Why should i share? Examining social capital and knowledge contribution in electronic networks of practice. *MIS Quarterly, 29*(S1), 35–57.

Wenger, E. (1998). *Communities of practice: Learning, meaning and identify*. Cambridge, UK: Cambridge University Press.

Wenger, E., McDermott, R., & Snyder, W. M. (2002). *Cultivating communities of practice (hardcover)*(1st ed.). Cambridge: Harvard Business Press.

y Gasset, J. O. (1961). *History as a system: And other essays toward a philosophy of history* (No. 122). WW Norton & Company.

Chapter 4
Empirical Evidence About Community Knowledge Preservation

Abstract This chapter reports case studies on four communities of practice in order to understand how a community preserves knowledge. The methodology of analysis used is the multiple case study, which is a qualitative method of research recognized as particularly suitable for exploring a phenomenon in a natural setting. The case studies reported allow me to better define the boundaries between the various processes of knowledge management by distinguishing the process of knowledge preservation from others. The case studies also provide evidence of the interplay between knowledge and knowing by clarifying the various mechanisms and tools that enable community members to select, store and actualize explicit and tacit forms of collective knowledge.

Keywords Communities of practice · Empirical evidence · Case study research · Knowledge preservation · Mechanisms and tools

4.1 The Case Study Method

This chapter reports four case studies on the scientific community of the Italian chapter of the Association of Information Systems (ItAIS); the religious community of Guardia Sanframondi; the religious community of Palermo; and the WoodenBoat community. The studies illustrate the process of knowledge preservation within a community of practice (CoP) and provide evidence about the main mechanisms and tools enabling these communities to preserve explicit and tacit forms of knowledge. The empirical evidence has been analyzed by using the case study method.

The term "case study" could lead to confusion because it has different meanings. It is used to describe both a "case," as unit of analysis, and a "research method." In what follows, I will use case study to refer to research method. Case study is one of the most frequently used research methods in social sciences (Yin 2013). A case study examines a phenomenon in its natural setting and collects data from one or a few entities, such as people, groups, or organizations (Benbasat et al. 1987;

© The Author(s) 2015
R. Agrifoglio, *Knowledge Preservation Through Community of Practice*,
SpringerBriefs in Information Systems, DOI 10.1007/978-3-319-22234-9_4

Yin 2004, 2013). Case study can mean single or multiple case studies. The latter simply includes two or more observations of the same framework, and overall is therefore regarded as being more robust (Yin 2004, 2013).

Although no single definition of the case study exists, the literature has tried to conceptualize this approach by comparing it with other research methods. As suggested by Yin (2004, p. 1), "Compared to other methods, the strength of the case study method is its ability to examine, in-depth, a 'case' within its 'real-life' context." Indeed, in respect of other methods, such as laboratory or field experiments, case study is not suitable when manipulation or control is involved. Table 4.1 provides a list of key characteristics of the case study method.

Besides defining the case study method, the literature agrees on when to use it. In particular, case study is recommended over other methods when two situations occur (Shavelson and Towne 2002; Yin 2004). It is used firstly when the form of the research question is explanatory, i.e. asking how or why something happens; and secondly, when scientists are willing to make direct observations and collect data in natural settings. Case study is a qualitative method particularly used in the IS field, since the object of IS research has shifted to organizational rather than technical issues (Benbasat et al. 1987; Myers and Avison 1997). To summarize, case study research is particularly well-suited to investigate a phenomenon when "research and theory are at their early, formative stages, and sticky, practice based problems where the experiences of the actors are important and the context of action is critical" (Benbasat et al. 1987, p. 369).

As explained before, the present study aims to understand how the CoP preserves knowledge. Although CoPs are recognized as a natural setting for the storage of knowledge over time, no study has tried to understand the process of knowledge preservation in such a community. In particular, previous research has linked CoP research and knowledge management literature by stressing mainly the creation and sharing of knowledge rather than its preservation. Knowledge preservation is often viewed as a process embedded into the wider processes of creation and sharing of knowledge. In contrast to previous research, this study explores how a community preserves knowledge by identifying the main mechanisms and tools enabling members to select, store and actualize the explicit and tacit forms of collective knowledge. It also explores the interplay between knowledge (as possession) and practice (as action), showing how a particular social and relational context, like that of CoP, enables members to preserve knowledge.

In this regard, the four empirical studies reported in this chapter take into account the methodological prescriptions of case study research in terms of research proposition, unit of analysis, novelty of the phenomena under inquiry, and criticality of context. Data were mainly collected from two types of sources: (1) internet websites (e.g., community websites; community forums and blogs; community documents; internet searches); and (2) scientific references.

The next sections describe the cases of the scientific community of the ItAIS, the religious community of Guardia Sanframondi, the religious community of Palermo, and the WoodenBoat community. The chapter ends with the discussion of results in the paragraph headed "Conclusions and Implications."

Table 4.1 Key characteristics of the case study

1	Phenomenon is examined in a natural setting
2	Data are collected by multiple means
3	One or few entities (person, group, or organization) are examined
4	The complexity of the unit is studied intensively
5	Case studies are more suitable for the exploration, classification and hypothesis development stages of the knowledge building process; the investigator should have a receptive attitude towards exploration
6	No experimental controls or manipulation are involved
7	The investigator may not specify the set of independent and dependent variables in advance
8	The results derived depend heavily on the integrative powers of the investigator
9	Changes in site selection and data collection methods could take place as the investigator develops new hypotheses
10	Case research is useful in the study of "why" and "how" questions because these deal with operational links to be traced over time rather than with frequency or incidence
11	The focus is on the contemporary events

Source Benbasat et al. 1987, p. 371

4.2   The Case of the Scientific Community of the ItAIS

The ItAIS[1] is the Italian chapter of the Association for Information Systems (AIS), a scientific community of academics and practitioners involved in the domain of Information Systems (IS). It is a community that aims to advance knowledge and promote excellence in the practice and study of information systems field.[2] As explained in the AIS mission statement, it is composed of individuals and organizations around the world interested in research, teaching, practice and study in Information Systems. Nowadays, the AIS community has members from over 90 countries belonging to three different geographical regions: Region 1, which includes the Americas; Region 2 for Europe, the Middle East and Africa; and Region 3 covering Asia and the Pacific.

The ItAIS scientific community was established in June 2003 in Naples during the European Conference on Information Systems (ECIS) by prominent Italian researchers actively engaged in the advancement of knowledge in the domain of business information systems. Among them should be noted Professors Claudio Ciborra, Alessandro D'Atri and Marco De Marco, who helped establish and develop the IS discipline in Italy.

The ItAIS aims to promote "the exchange of ideas, experiences, and knowledge among scholars and professionals engaged in the development, management, and

---

[1]This paragraph was written by Rocco Agrifoglio and Davide De Gennaro.

[2]http://aisnet.org/?AboutAIS (Accessed 15 May 2015).

use of information and communication systems and technology in both private and public Italian organizations".[3] To achieve the community aim, ItAIS was designed to support community members in performing their practice through the following organizational structure and procedures.

The Executive Board, comprising a group of community members, aimed to lead the scientific community by defining organizational and management issues, scheduling annual meetings, and sharing information among community members. The community works through five ad hoc Special Interest Groups (SIGs).[4] The SIG is a research group where community members spontaneously decide to join together to share an interest in advancing a specific area of knowledge in IS. More generally, as suggested on the AIS website, SIGs are "dedicated to researching, developing and disseminating knowledge based on vast experiences of specific topics in the management and organization of IS".[5] The ItAIS's SIGs are: eHealth and Social eServices (EHSES); Open Business Models and Service Science (OPSE); Research Quality in Information Systems—Theories and Methodologies (ReQuIS-TheMe); e-Leadership Development for a Digitized World (ISEdu); and Digital Accounting (DIGAC).[6]

The ItAIS community also encourages the interaction and exchange of ideas, experiences and knowledge among members by promoting meetings, such as the annual conference of ItAIS and other workshops and seminars in the IS field[7]; and the use of IT-assisted tools, such as the ItAIS community on LinkedIn.[8]

In particular, the annual conference of ItAIS aims to stimulate debate on the current trends in IS among national and international scholars, who participate by presenting and discussing papers in parallel sessions. Figure 4.1 shows the most attractive tracks of the ItAIS annual conference over the last years (2011 in Rome; 2012 in Rome; 2013 in Milan; 2014 in Genova).

Figure 4.1 shows that the ItAIS annual conference's more attractive tracks from 2011 to 2014 are: Accounting Information Systems (AIS); Organizational Change and Impacts of ICT (ORGICT); e-Services and Social Networks, Virtual Organizations and Smartcities (ESERV); Human-Computer Interaction (HCI); and Information Systems, Innovation Transfer, and new Business Models (ISITBM). These results point out an ongoing participation in the conference tracks and a multidisciplinary research themes over time. Furthermore, Fig. 4.2 shows the ItAIS annual conference attendance figures in terms of numbers of programme committee, paper submissions and authors from 2011 to 2014.

---

[3]http://ais.site-ym.com/members/group.aspx?id=101636 (Accessed 15 May 2015).

[4]http://ais.site-ym.com/members/group_content_view.asp?group=101636&id=166578 (Accessed 15 May 2015).

[5]http://aisnet.org/?SpecialInterestGroup (Accessed 15 May 2015).

[6]http://ais.site-ym.com/members/group_content_view.asp?group=101636&id=166578 (Accessed 15 May 2015).

[7]http://ais.site-ym.com/members/group_content_view.asp?group=101636&id=166658 (Accessed 15 May 2015).

[8]http://www.linkedin.com/grp/home?gid=4140068 (Accessed 16 May 2015).

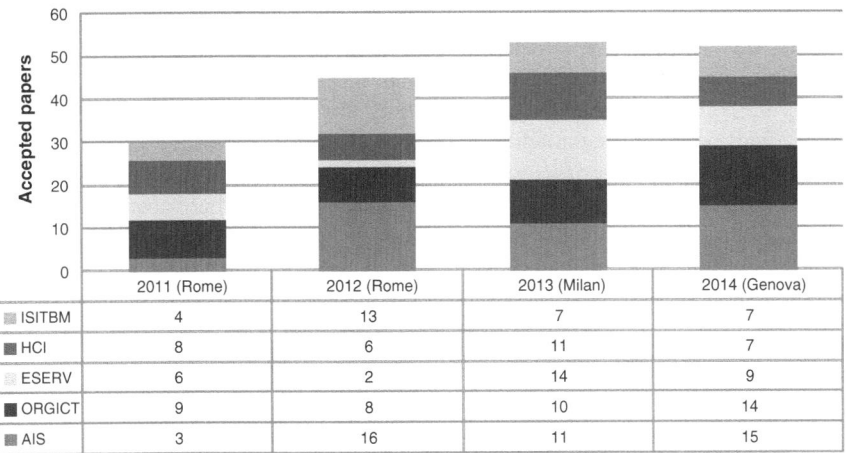

Fig. 4.1 The ItAIS conference's most attractive tracks

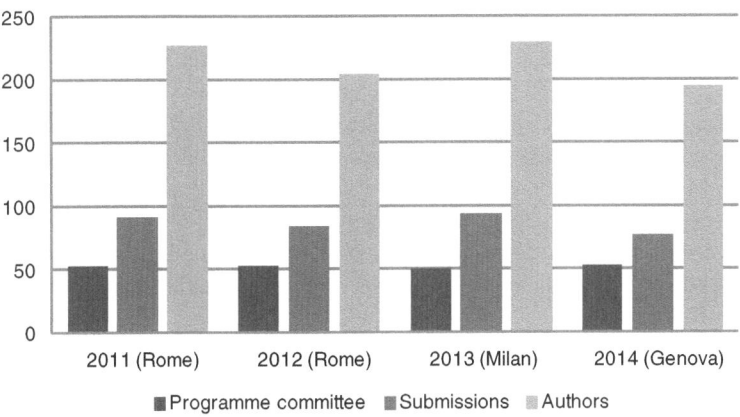

Fig. 4.2 The ItAIS conference's attendance figures

Figure 4.2 points out that community members effectively take part in the ItAIS annual conference. Such result arises from the ItAIS board and track chairs who have allowed IS scholars and practitioners to participate in the conference activities, so providing a good relevance of the conference across the various editions. Besides the ItAIS annual conference, this community also promotes other interesting events, such as the Terracina Research Workshop, Piacenza Day and Alpine Seminar Information Systems, and is actively involved in supporting the development of the Mediterranean Conference on Information Systems (MCIS). These meetings offer community members various advantages. First, they allow members to discuss and share their research with others in order to obtain advice and feedback useful for advancing knowledge in their specific research topic both before (papers accepted at conferences are double-blind reviewed) and during the conference. Moreover, they stimulate community members to establish new relationships and strengthen old ones, thus creating the conditions for future academic collaboration. Finally, papers presented at the meetings are usually stored in the conference/workshop proceedings, enabling community members to preserve knowledge and retrieve it when they need to. For instance, the ItAIS annual meeting usually publishes a selection of its best papers in a Springer volume, while the other papers presented at the conference are published in the conference proceedings. In addition, ItAIS community members, and AIS members in general, have free access to the eLibrary, one of the larger online libraries in the IS field. This portal provides excellent access to numerous magazines and enables members to follow up on conference proceedings.

Finally, since December 2011 community members have a group on LinkedIn, named "ItAIS—The Italian Association for Information Systems," to support social relationships and knowledge exchange. It especially serves the SIGs. Apart from the ItAIS website and those of the various conferences, the ItAIS's LinkedIn group is the only IT-assisted tool that enables community members to discuss issues among themselves, in particular, issues arising from their practice.

Nowadays, the ItAIS community is composed of about 120 members from multiple disciplines, such as management, engineering, informatics, sociology and psychology, of whom 117 are academics and practitioners.

More generally, ItAIS community members interact with each other to exchange the information, knowledge and experiences needed to develop their practice. The SIGs, the ItAIS annual conference and other meetings are some examples of how the community supports social and professional relationships in order to create, share and store knowledge among its members. As explained by Spagnoletti (2013, p. 1), ItAIS is a "stimulating and suitable arena for sharing and enriching their research endeavors within, and often beyond, their primary areas of interest."

4.3   The Case of Two Religious Communities of the *Confederazione dell'Oratorio di San Filippo Neri*

The *confederazione dell'oratorio di San Filippo Neri*[9] (Confederation of the Oratory of Saint Philip Neri) is a religious confederation bringing together congregations that have grown over time since the first was established in 1575. These congregations, which numbered about 300 in the past, were completely autonomous and united solely by spiritual and common ideals, as approved by the *Constitutiones* of Pope Paul V in 1612, until the community was officially established under the name of the *Institutum Oratorii S. Philippi Nerii* in 1933 and

---

[9]This paragraph was written by Rocco Agrifoglio and Nicola Albanese.

Confoederatio Oratorii S. Philippi Nerii in 1969 (Cerrato n.d.). Nowadays, the *confederazione dell'oratorio di San Filippo Neri* is composed of 86 religious communities, named "*congregazioni*" (congregations), located in 20 countries. This study will focus on two of these communities: the *congregazione dell'oratorio di Guardia Sanframondi* (the congregation of Guardia Sanframondi) and the *congregazione dell'oratorio di Palermo* (the congregation of Palermo).

4.3.1 The Religious Community of Guardia Sanframondi

The *congregazione dell'oratorio di Guardia Sanframondi* is one of the most important congregations of the *confederazione dell'oratorio di San Filippo Neri*. It was originally founded by Father Marzio Piccirillo, who was also a saint and a prominent member of this community, in Guardia Sanframondi.[10] The latter is a small village located in the Campania Region of Italy, in the Benevento Province, that is now comprises 5,341 inhabitants.

In 1626 Saint Philip Neri was confirmed as the patron saint of Guardia Sanframondi, and soon thereafter the first secular oratory for men was founded. The newly established religious community was inspired to live an especially profound and intense Christian life. Then another religious institution, named The Philippine Virgins, was created in Guardia Sanframondi for unmarried women seeking to serve the Lord. In 1636, thanks to the decree of Diocesan Bishop Sigismondo Gambacorta, the *congregazione dell'oratorio di Guardia Sanframondi* was officially established. The community aimed to give absolute dedication in service to their fellow man. The community members (known as oratorians) were dedicated to serving society in terms of apostolic and social commitment in order to ease physical and moral suffering and reduce the spiritual and material evils which cause the marginalization of the disadvantaged.

More generally, this religious community characterized itself in its early years by a clear apostolic duty to society. The community members have recognized the need to give an adequate response to society's needs, and concentrated on alleviating the exploitation of minors and women in the workplace as well as the marginalization of the city's humblest and poorest inhabitants. Moreover, instead of depending on the Church and Christian charitable organizations, this community sought assistance, donations and guidance from its own community members in the 18th century. Thus, it aimed to assist those who were suffering, needy and defenseless, rather than to solve society's complex issues.

Following the positive example of their predecessors, current members of the *congregazione dell'oratorio di Guardia Sanframondi* serve local churches working with parochial catechesis and assisting traditional Catholic orders in order to promote devotion and to cultivate spiritual practices. It now includes non-ordained lay

---

[10]http://www.santuarioassunta.com/oratorio-a-guardia (Accessed 20 May 2015).

brothers as well as ordained priests who, spurred on by the spirit of goodness and altruism, are committed to spreading the Gospel through the joy, purity, and authenticity that define them. Through their vocation, the faithful of the Guardia Sanframondi religious community are today a concrete example of God's love.

Their religious practice has been handed down from one generation to the next over several centuries. Besides weekly rites, community members are also expected to hold various events, such feasts and religious anniversaries, which give greater meaning to their actions. For example, every seven years they hold the septennial rituals of penitence, which date from 1620. As an age-old tradition, the processions weaving throughout the streets of the village are the clearest evidence of a vibrant spirituality that is carried on with passion and the active participation of community members. The long and spectacular procession includes the Mysteries (more than 100 paintings depicting scenes from the Bible and from the life of the Church as interpreted by over 2,000 people); penitents with their white habit and hoods (over 500 flagellants whipping themselves till they bleed); and citizens from Guardia Sanframondi and the surrounding villages.[11] This ceremony is an expression of faith and renders homage to the Virgin, but it also serves to pass on the tradition to future generations. In the hope that this tradition continues to ignite profound faith in the new generation, the hooded penitents captivate spectators. The *Sanctuary Bulletin,*[12] first published in 1955, and also national and foreign publications from 1880 to the present day, gathers clear information about the ever-growing crowds of the faithful who participate in the Ritual of Penitence. It is a traditional tool, which allows members to share Saint Filippo's thought, religious programs and community initiatives. Figure 4.3 shows sections of one of the first editions of the *Sanctuary Bulletin* of the *congregazione dell'oratorio di Guardia Sanframondi.*

The community also cultivates the practice of daily routines, such as masses, morning prayers and hymns, vespers and the adoration of the Eucharist. Furthermore, the *congregazione dell'oratorio di Guardia Sanframondi* has decided to use IT-assisted tools to encourage social and spiritual participation among members and improve communication among them. In particular, besides the traditional Sanctuary Bulletin, the community has created an official website,[13] a Facebook fan page[14] and a Twitter account.[15] The official website has received over 1,500,000 visits, including 18,600 in the last month and 1,660 in the last week. IT-assisted tools not only promote the Gospel, but provide people, especially the young, with the chance to get to know the community's activities and news. Moreover, the community has created a live TV channel[16] for sharing and storing the various celebrations, festivals and Christians rituals in which all community

[11]http://www.santuarioassunta.com/la-storia-dei-riti (Accessed 20 May 2015).

[12]http://www.santuarioassunta.com/bollettino/bollettini (Accessed 20 May 2015).

[13]http://www.santuarioassunta.com/ (Accessed 20 May 2015).

[14]https://www.facebook.com/SantuarioAssuntaGuardiaSanframondi (Accessed 20 May 2015).

[15]https://twitter.com/SantAssunta (Accessed 20 May 2015).

[16]http://www.santuarioassunta.com/live-tv/non-categorizzato/live-tv (Accessed 20 May 2015).

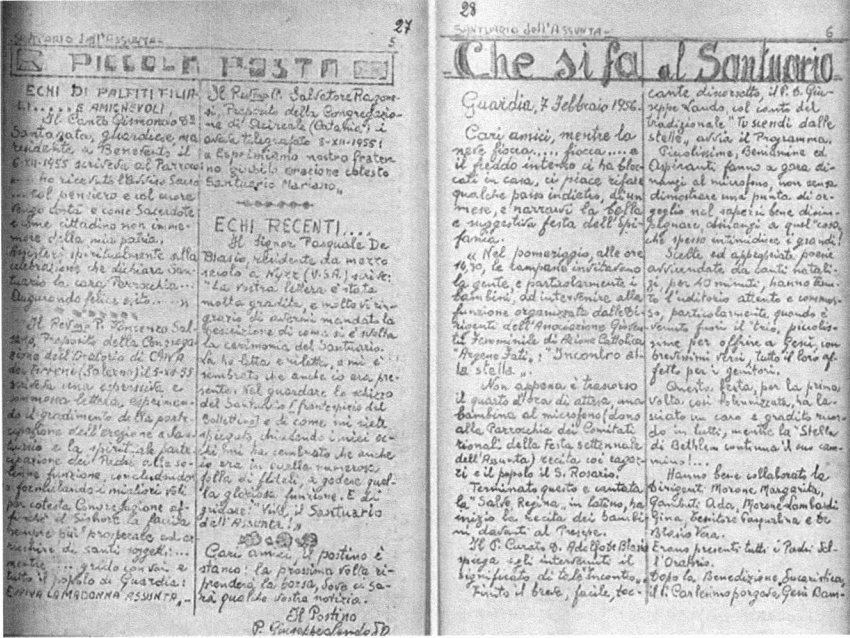

Fig. 4.3 An image from the sanctuary bulletin of the *congregazione dell'oratorio di Guardia Sanframondi* dated February 1956 [http://www.santuarioassunta.com/bollettino/bollettini/anno-1956/bollettino-febbraio-1956 (Accessed 20 May 2015)]

members are engaged. Every celebration is broadcast live with the possibility of interacting with the Fathers of the Oratory as well as other viewers during the live broadcasts. Through online chats, it is also possible to send messages and comment on the various events. Also in the repertoire is a video library where a dedicated link allows anyone to view past events and ceremonies. IT-assisted tools enable community members to communicate and interact among themselves, so representing an alternative and more effective way to stay up to date and present in community life.

4.3.2 The Religious Community of Palermo

The *congregazione dell'oratorio di San Filippo Neri—Padri Filippini—di Palermo* has been in existence since 1593.[17] In 1952, Father Pietro Bozzo, a member of the Oratory of Rome established by Father Filippo Neri, and other priests, decided to retreat into the Church of San Pietro Martire in Palermo to

---

[17]http://oratoriosanfilipponeripalermo.org/ (Accessed 21 May 2015).

perform their spiritual practice in seclusion. They aimed to achieve saintliness, follow evangelical teaching, embrace religious life and pursue personal sanctification. During this period, Father Pietro Bozzo explained to other priests the model of Father Filippo Neri's Oratory, in which people lived a holy and penitent life, devoting themselves entirely to the salvation of souls. Inspired by this spiritual model, they decided to create in the heart of Palermo an oratory based on the example of Father Filippo Neri. In 1953, after Father Filippo's model was approved, the priests established in Palermo the *congregazione dell'oratorio dei Padri Filippini.*[18]

The *congregazione dell'oratorio di Palermo* was not a community-based project, nor did it result from a series of initiatives. Rather, it was inspired by the life of the priest, Filippo, who was rich in humanity and lacked any clerical influences. In contrast to the original objective, community members were no longer enveloped in seclusion, removed from the world, and solely dedicated to contemplation. Rather, they were now intent on living an evangelical life in the service of others.

This new model of religious life inspired community members to work for their fellow man. Thus, the religious community cultivated its spiritual practice in keeping with ancient traditions through the simple reading of the Gospel, prayer, ceremonies and various popular events. But it also included additional services to others, such as helping the sick; providing spiritual, moral and material assistance to the incarcerated; aiding drug addicts; assisting women and vulnerable girls seeking escape from exploitation; helping orphans, the elderly and the neglected; improving literacy for the blind and deaf; and opening schools for village and country children. More generally, the community tried to tackle the societal issues of the most needy and defenseless by responding to an evangelical calling.

Initially, the *congregazione dell'oratorio di San Filippo Neri—Padri Filippini —di Palermo* was not organized as a typical oratory. The community did not have a list of members, nor charters that imposed rules, but simply comprised a group of ordained priests and lay individuals who followed in the footsteps of Father Filippo Neri. In this regard, members aimed to cultivate community practice together through prayer and brotherly cooperation in works of faith. Since joining the community was free, numerous priests and lay people who lived close to the community decided to participate in congregational activities. Shortly after, the religious community decided to purchase the Church of Santa Rosalia, the patron saint of Palermo, because the ancient Church of San Pietro Martire was proving very small for the many activities of the members.

Nowadays, the community comprises the Church priests and about 30 lay people of all ages, actively engaged in performing community activities. In particular, the community fathers celebrate the sacraments and administer confession, as well as offering spiritual direction. They also serve the sick, ensuring that they receive physical, moral and spiritual care. Lay people support the priests in carrying out their activities, so effectively working in the service of the community and society.

---

[18]http://oratoriosanfilipponeripalermo.org/congregazione/storia/ (Accessed 21 May 2015).

They are an example to anyone who wishes to join the *congregazione dell'oratorio di San Filippo Neri—Padri Filippini—di Palermo*. Such dedication passes naturally and spontaneously from older to younger generations through community practice.

In order to better explain the community activities done by members, Table 4.2 shows a typical day for members of the *congregazione dell'oratorio di San Filippo Neri—Padri Filippini—di Palermo*.

As Table 4.2 shows, the fathers celebrate daily masses, morning prayer and hymns, Vespers and the Adorations of the Eucharist, while the free time is spent in prayer, study and serving the community. Lay members effectively serve by working in the community.

Members have also decided to use IT-assisted tools for sharing information about the community and its initiatives, and for promoting Saint Filippo Neri's message. In particular, IT-assisted tools include the official website[19] and a Facebook fan page,[20] which are regularly visited by the faithful. IT-assisted tools are also used to promote the ancient "house of the fathers" of the congregation, which has become the center of the regional archaeological Antonio Salinas museum.[21] This historical building from the 16th century holds one of the richest collections of artifacts of Italy's Punic and Greek eras. It also owns books, manuscripts, presses, photographs, sarcophagi, memorial stones, bronzes, personal artifacts and coins that are, to a great extent, testimony to Sicilian history and devotion.

4.4 The Case of the WoodenBoat Community

The WoodenBoat is an online CoP consisting of owners,[22] admirers, builders, and designers of wooden boats.[23] Founded in September 1974 by Jon Wilson, this community started as an American magazine for boat amateurs. The founder assembled the magazine from his cabin in North Brooksville, Maine without using electricity or plumbing. The first issue of the magazine was a great success, so much so that Wilson sold about 400 individual copies and signed up 200 subscribers. Figure 4.4 shows Issue 1 of the WoodenBoat Magazine, printed in 1974.

Then, thanks to the growing number of owners, builders, designers and general boat enthusiasts, what began as a simple magazine became an important place for sharing information and knowledge about old and new wooden boats. Thus was

---

[19]http://oratoriosanfilipponeripalermo.org/ (Accessed 21 May 2015).

[20]https://www.facebook.com/oratoriosanfilipponeripalermo (Accessed 21 May 2015).

[21]http://www.regione.sicilia.it/beniculturali/salinas/ (Accessed 18 April 2015).

[22]This paragraph is based on and extends some elements of the analyses developed by the author in Agrifoglio and Metallo (2015).

[23]http://www.woodenboat.com/community (Accessed 23 May 2015).

Table 4.2 A typical day for members of the *congregazione dell'oratorio di San Filippo Neri—Padri Filippini—di Palermo*

Time	Schedule of events
7:00 am	Reading and morning prayers
7:45 am	Breakfast
12:45 pm	Mid-day with community meditation
1:15 pm	Meal including brief reading from Sacred Scripture
1:45 pm	Fraternal moment
6:00 pm	Holy Rosary prayer with the faithful
6:30 pm	Eucharistic celebration including Vespers prayer
8:00 pm	Dinner, including a brief spiritual reading
8:45 pm	Fraternal moment

Source The website of the Oratorio di San Filippo Neri di Palermo [http://oratoriosanfilipponeripalermo.org/congregazione/una-giornata-tipo/ (Accessed 21 May 2015)]

Fig. 4.4 The WoodenBoat magazine, volume 1, number 1 in Sept/Oct 1974 [http://www.woodenboatstore.com/product/WoodenBoat_magazine_DIGITAL_Issue_1/woodenboat_1-30 (Accessed 23 May 2015)]

VOLUME 1, NUMBER 1   SEPTEMBER/OCTOBER 1974 $3.00

born the WoodenBoat, an online community that enables members to share their interest and passion for building wooden boats.

Boat-building is one of the most ancient and difficult branches of engineering. Although a traditional wooden boat can be built by using common DIY tools such as hammers, cross-cut saws, power drills, benches and vices, the specific knowledge and building techniques needed for doing such activity mean this work is not suitable for everyone. Building a boat is a very complex task that requires knowledge of materials, tools and processing techniques, but above all a great deal of experience. In the past, within indigenous communities the knowledge of what a boat is and how to build one was rooted in the community itself and articulated across the various generations by practice (Ward 2006). For instance, with reference to wooden-boat building in early Egypt, Ward (2006, p. 120) stated: "Unlike any other tradition, however, Egyptian boat-builders lashed planks together across the hull, rather than along plank edges, in a unique transfer of technology. It can be suggested that the practices by which the transition was accomplished were rapidly standardized and can be traced through Egyptian boat-building for more than a thousand years." Figure 4.5 shows some ancient Egyptian wooden-boat building scenes.

Although wooden-boat building still goes on, few people possess the knowledge needed to do it. Among these, the WoodenBoat community plays a crucial role in sharing and storing knowledge of techniques, tools, and processes, so enabling members to cultivate their practice.

Nowadays, this community reaches owners, builders, designers and general wooden-boat enthusiasts by using traditional and IT-assisted tools, such as a website, which is composed of online magazines, forum and blog, thematic events, photo and video gallery, and web TV, and social networks, such as a Facebook fan page.

The WoodenBoat website allows people to join the community and its forum; to chat; and to get information about old and new wooden boats as well as traditional methods of boat design, construction and repair.[24] Furthermore, the website contains an ad hoc section kept updated to promote events such as the Boat-Building and Rowing Challenge, WoodenBoat Regatta Series, WOOD Regatta, and WoodenBoat Show.

WoodenBoat Publications encompass different magazines and books such as *WoodenBoat* magazine; *Professional BoatBuilder* magazine; *Small Boats* magazine; etc..[25] Among these, the *WoodenBoat* magazine is the first and most widely read journal, published six times each year and now over 30 years in publication, for wooden-boat owners, beginner builders, boating enthusiasts, builders, designers, repairers and surveyors. Another important magazine is *Professional BoatBuilder*, published six times a year, which focuses on materials, design, construction techniques and repair solutions chosen by marine professionals.

The WoodenBoat forum allows people to get information about specific topics such as building/repair, designs/plans, people and places, *WoodenBoat* magazine, tools/materials/techniques/products and miscellaneous boat-related subjects.[26] As statistics suggest, the WoodenBoat forum is widely used, with 164,247 threads, 3,158,888 posts and 36,385 members. WoodenBoat community members also use

[24]http://www.woodenboat.com (Accessed 23 May 2015).

[25]http://www.woodenboat.com/woodenboat-publications-brooklin-maine (Accessed 23 May 2015).

[26]http://www.forum.woodenboat.com (Accessed 23 May 2015).

(a)   **(b)**

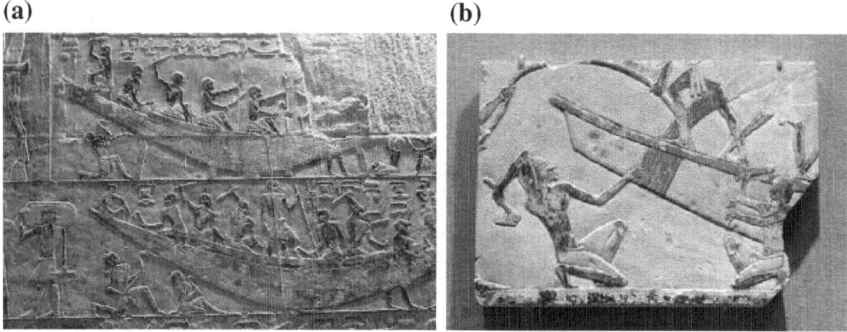

Fig. 4.5 Ancient Egyptians Wooden-Boat building scenes. *Source* (1) Werner (2011) and (2) Wilbour (n.d.)

the blog[27] to post stories about and adventures with boats as well as other information identified as particularly relevant for boat amateurs.

Furthermore, the WoodenBoat website contains a photo- and video-gallery section[28] and WoodenBoat TV,[29] a collection of short and long movies on wooden-boat design, construction and repair. The movies collected in the video gallery and WoodenBoat TV sections are a very useful guide for community members carrying on their practice as their work or hobby. Thanks to these movies, community members learn from expert practitioners the old techniques and methods of making wooden boats, so promoting the sharing and preservation of know-how.

Finally, the community has also created the official Facebook fan page of the WoodenBoat.[30] The WoodenBoat fan page has over 100,000 likes and about 9,000 boat enthusiasts talking about it.

4.5 Conclusions and Implications

The case studies reported provide valuable evidence about explicit and tacit forms of collective knowledge preservation in CoPs.

First, they provide evidence about the processes of knowledge preservation, showing the commonalities, differences and interplay between preservation and the other processes of knowledge management, such as knowledge creation and sharing. All the case studies reported point out how knowledge preservation is

---

[27]http://boats.woodenboat.com/ (Accessed 23 May 2015).

[28]http://www.wood-enboat.com/photo-video-gallery (Accessed 23 May 2015).

[29]http://www.wood-enboat.com/woodenboat-tv (Accessed 23 May 2015).

[30]https://www.facebook.com/WoodenBoatPub?fref=ts (Accessed 24 May 2015).

critical in knowledge management because it is the beginning and end of the whole process of managing knowledge. For instance, the scientific community of the ItAIS clearly shows how community members exploit preserved collective knowledge (existing theories, methods and research tools) to create new knowledge (contributions) that, once stored, will form the basis for future research. Similarly, the WoodenBoat community enables members to acquire information on the materials, tools and processing techniques needed for building a boat because such knowledge has previously been embedded into traditional and IT-assisted tools. The two religious communities of Guardia Sanframondi and Palermo, on the other hand, mostly illustrate how repeating a set of activities over time in a social context of interaction allows members to transfer knowledge across generations. Within communities, knowledge is drawn from the context of where people are and what they contribute to, because collective knowledge enables members to perform a set of coordinated activities necessary for doing a specific task. Also, doing such activities allows a community, and community members in particular, to create and share new knowledge, which will then be selected and stored. In respect of knowledge creation and sharing, preserving knowledge thus refers to the process of the selection, storage, and actualization of explicit and tacit forms of knowledge.

The case studies reported also provide evidence of the interplay between knowledge (epistemology of possession) and knowing (epistemology of practice). As explained in Chap. 3, a CoP is a social context in which practice comes from explicit and tacit forms of collective knowledge and contributes to the latter thanks to the interaction that community members have with each other and with the world (Brown and Cook 1999). While knowledge is static, knowing is constituted every day in the ongoing and contextual practice of community members. It is socially constituted and deeply rooted in the shared repertoire of the community, even if its members are geographically dispersed (Orlikowski 2002). The case of the religious communities of Guardia Sanframondi and Palermo shows this clearly, as their shared repertoire, consisting of community routines, shared norms, religious artifacts and vocabulary, enables members to perform social actions, while such repertoire is also the result of these social actions. Similarly, the other two communities, i.e. the scientific community of the ItAIS and the WoodenBoat community, also highlight how carrying out a specific practice in a context of interaction helps to preserve collective knowledge in community-shared repertoire. Building upon the practice-based approach (e.g., Carlile 2002; Corradi et al. 2010; Nicolini et al. 2003; Schiavone and Agrifoglio 2012; Agrifoglio and Metallo 2015), case studies reported clearly show that sociality exists not only with other human beings, but also with artifacts. Indeed, knowledge is a factor of organizational life that may be enacted and reproduced by practices in a social context, and in a community in particular. Following the Carlile's (2002) thought, I also believe that CoP is a natural setting that enables its members to structure knowledge in "objects" (artifacts that individuals work with) and "ends" (outcomes that demonstrate success in creating, measuring, or manipulating objects) that are of consequence in a given community practice. In this regard, the shared repertoire of a

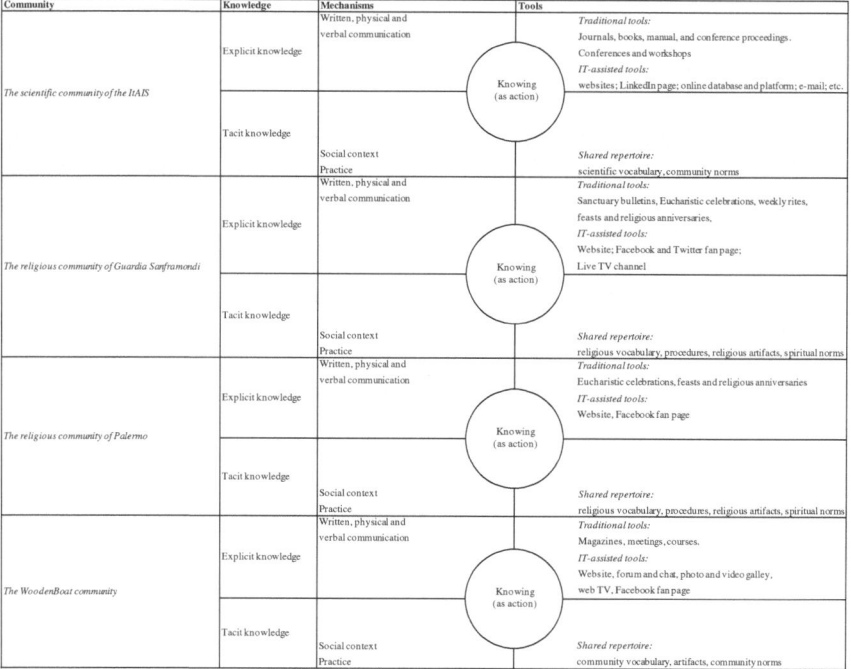

Fig. 4.6 Mechanisms and tools for preserving knowledge

community is both the medium for and the outcome of the reproduction of practices.

Finally, the case studies reported also demonstrate the mechanisms and tools enabling members to preserve explicit and tacit forms of collective knowledge. Figure 4.6 shows the main mechanisms and tools used by these CoPs for preserving knowledge.

As Fig. 4.6 shows, although these communities are characterized by the performance of different practices, the mechanisms and tools used for preserving explicit and tacit forms of collective knowledge are similar. In particular, while some differences are found in the tools used to preserve explicit and tacit knowledge, the mechanisms enabling such CoPs to select, store and actualize explicit and tacit knowledge seem be the same. However, the tools used for preserving knowledge simply depend on the different choices and activities of a single community at a specific point in time. Over time, in fact, they could change. Apart the differences, much more interesting are the commonalities among the mechanisms and the interplay between knowing and knowledge. While the methodological prescriptions for case studies require us to exercise caution in generalizing the results, it can be argued that, within the CoPs investigated, the main mechanisms enabling collective knowledge preservation are written, physical and verbal communication for explicit knowledge, and social context and practice for tacit knowledge. The CoP is a natural setting where social relationships enable members to perform a set of coordinated activities necessary for doing a task. Practice in a social context is not only what people do, but also the locus for the production and reproduction of social relationships. In this regard, as Gherardi (2000) stated, while knowledge enables members to perform a practice, it is also constructed by practicing in a context of interaction.

References

Agrifoglio, R., & Metallo, C. (2015). Preserving knowledge through community of practice: A multiple case study. In L. Mola, F. Pennarola & S. Za (Eds.), *From information to smart society* (Vol. 5, pp. 103–111). Lecture Notes in Information Systems and Organisation (LNISO), Springer.

Benbasat, I., Goldstein, D. K., & Mead, M. (1987). The case research strategy in studies of information systems. *MIS Quarterly, 11*(3), 369–386.

Brown, J. S., & Cook, S. D. N. (1999). Bridging epistemologies: The generative dance between organizational knowledge and organizational knowing. *Organization Science, 10*(4), 381–400.

Carlile, P. R. (2002). A pragmatic view of knowledge and boundaries: Boundary objects in new product development. *Organization Science, 13*(4), 442–455.

Cerrato, E. A. (n.d.). *Benvenuti.* http://www.oratoriosanfilippo.org/presentazione.html. Accessed May 20, 2015.

Corradi, G., Gherardi, S., & Verzelloni, L. (2010). Through the practice lens: Where is the bandwagon of practice-based studies heading? *Management Learning, 41*(3), 265–283.

Gherardi, S. (2000). Practice-based theorizing on learning and knowing in organizations: An introduction. *Organization, 7*(2), 211–223.

Myers, M. D., & Avison, D. (1997). Qualitative research in information systems. *Management Information Systems Quarterly, 21,* 241–242.

Nicolini, D., Gherardi, S., & Yanow, D. (2003). *Knowing in organizations: A Practice-based Approach.* USA: M. E. Sharpe Inc.

Orlikowski, W. J. (2002). Knowing in practice: Enacting a collective capability in distributed organizing. *Organization Science, 13*(3), 249–273.

Schiavone, F., & Agrifoglio, R. (2012). Communities of practice and practice preservation: A case study. In M. De Marco, D. Te'eni, V. Albano & S. Za, *Information systems: Crossroads for organization, management, accounting and engineering.* Berlin: Springer.

Shavelson, R., & Towne, L. (2002). *Scientific inquiry in education.* Washington, DC: National Academy Press. Shavelson Scientific inquiry in education 2002.

Spagnoletti, P. (2013). Introduction. In P. Spagnoletti (Ed.), *Organizational change and information systems: Working and living together in new ways.* Lecture Notes in Information Systems and Organisation (LNISO): Springer.

Ward, C. (2006). Boat-building and its social context in early Egypt: Interpretations from the First Dynasty boat-grave cemetery at Abydos. *Antiquity, 80*(307), 118–129.

Werner, B. (2011). Egyptian boats, Saqqara (Ägypten, Sakkara, Mastaba des Ti). Photograph. *Wikimedia Commons.* Source: Saqqara_BW_11.jpg. Web. 24 July 2011. http://commons.wikimedia.org/wiki/File:Saqqara_BW_11_c.jpg. Accessed 16 March 2015.

Wilbour, C. E. (n.d.). *Boat-Building scene* (ca. 664–634 B.C.E). Brooklyn Museum, Charles Edwin Wilbour Fund, 51.14. Creative Commons-BY. https://www.brooklynmuseum.org/opencollection/objects/3553/Boat-Building_Scene (Accessed 21 May 2015).

Yin, R. K. (2004). *The case study anthology.* Beverly Hills: Sage publications.

Yin, R. K. (2013). *Case study research: Design and methods.* Beverly Hills: Sage publications.